Mindful Money

*How to Overcome the Number-One
Enemy of Financial Success:*
Your Brain

CRAIG VERDI

Mindful Money

Published by More Cowbell Books, LLC.
Available in paperback from Amazon.com, CreateSpace.com, and other retail outlets.

ISBN 978-0-9860538-7-0 (Paperback)

Book design by Jane Gerke

This publication has been compiled based on personal experience, research, and the author's opinion, but it is not intended to replace legal, financial, or other professional advice or services. Every reasonable attempt has been made to provide accurate content, and the author and publisher disclaim responsibility for any errors or omissions contained herein. The samples provided are for educational and discussion purposes only. All website addresses cited were current at the time of publication. Any trademarks, service marks, product names or named features are assumed to be the property of their respective owners and are used solely for editorial reference, not endorsement. Past performance is not indicative of future results. The charts and material shown in this publication do not constitute a solicitation to buy or sell any securities whatsoever. Always consider all publicly available fundamental and technical data before making any investment.

CONTENTS

"Craig Verdi has written an easy-to-understand guide to financial success. His message is clear: Turn off the news, turn off your brain. As he says, investing is a project for decades, not days."

—Bill Buckner, *former Major League Baseball player*

"I just finished reading the first edition of Craig Verdi's newest book *Mindful Money* and I must say it could be one of the most thorough, thought-provoking, and insightful financial planning publications I've seen in my 40 years of being on Wall Street.

"I first met Craig in the 1980s and very soon entrusted him to personally manage my family's portfolios and estate planning, as we do to this day. His dedication to his profession, his clients' success and welfare is incredible in a world consisting of salespeople and robo-advisors.

"Take some time to read Craig's valuable insights and see the how his direction and advice may help you achieve every one of your financial dreams…and then share it with your friends and family who you value the most. I'm confident they'll thank you many times over!"

—Edward A. Bondy, *ETF Consultant,*
Founder & CEO of Aviara Wealth Advisors, FINRA Series 7, 24, 63, 65

"It's behavioral finance explained in a manner that most people will understand. In a world where our eyes and ears are glued to CNBC or Bloomberg—a continual source of overwhelming information to the point where good decisions are no longer made—*Mindful Money* does an excellent job framing what the real issues are with building wealth. It's simple to understand and it's easy once you get it—and this book tells you how to do it."

—Ben James, CFA, CFP®,
Portfolio Manager & Investment Analyst, Elevate Wealth Advisors

---

"This book addresses very well the needs of two types of investor: For the new investor, the author draws from over 30 years of his own experience and the wisdom of other well-known investors. Craig points us to the fundamental problem we all face in starting our financial journey: finding a fiduciary advisor and then getting out of our own way. For experienced/successful investors, this book lends comfort to experienced investors (including me) who have followed the basic advice of the author and made money in the process."

—Steven D. Maurer, Ph.D.,
Emeritus Professor of Management, Old Dominion University

INTRODUCTION

With thousands of books available on investing, why read another? My goal in the following pages is to add a fresh perspective and give you practical and actionable investing advice that *sticks*. I do not put the blame for poor investment results on the market, your advisor, the government, or even the dreaded Federal Reserve.

I believe that we investors—not investments—are the key ingredient to our success. We do not need to change investments or find new investment ideas. *We need to change ourselves to be successful.* I see investors continually sabotaging their long-term goals with bad decisions that are based on short-term events. *Mindful Money* will show you a way around that problem.

If you wanted to learn about World War II, you might start by reading the stories of Eisenhower, Roosevelt, Churchill, MacArthur, Patton, and Truman. In the process, however, you could get sidetracked into reading conspiracy theories about how Hitler escaped to Argentina. (One such book, *Grey Wolf*, stretches almost 400 pages. It is well written by a very intelligent guy, but the easier and more plausible story still lies with Hitler dead in a bunker in Berlin.) This is exactly how we get sidetracked, confused, and frustrated with investing. We set out to get helpful information, only to be become sidetracked by a captivating narrative of how we can get rich quick if we listen to a secret story, or how the market is rigged against us and we need to get at the "real information."

Why are we so easily drawn away by the obscure? Why are conspiracy theories so much more enjoyable than reality? Why will some people devour such nonsense as "The 10 Secrets to Playing the Options that Wall Street Doesn't Want You To Know," when they can read lasting wisdom from such great investors as Peter Lynch, Benjamin Graham, or Warren Buffett?

For whatever reason, we are not equipped to think rationally. By definition, if you thought rationally in every situation, you would be omniscient: No question would pose a conundrum for you. You would spend a lot less time selecting petunias or oven cleaner. You would never get to know the big, semi-scary guy with all the tattoos at Home Depot. Life would be dull. We would have no debates, no conversations, or any of the normal joys of human life if we thought rationally. Every time you mentioned something to someone to start a conversation they would say, "Yes, I know." It would be like talking to Spock from *Star Trek*.

I have been accused of having a strange way of thinking about things and I fear that people are right. For all practical purposes, I can't think of what life was like before my introduction to the search engine. I used to sit around thinking about such burning issues as running out of music and why there isn't generic WD-40.

I have always had a different view of investing. I don't think my view should be unusual, but it is. The term *contrarian investor* has come to mean an investor who buys stocks that are out of favor and represent an unusually good value at precisely the time no one wants them. To me, that's not contrarian—they are simply doing the most rational thing possible!

It takes patience and nerves to become successful, and greed will drive the great majority to opt for the simple story in which you get rich quick, instead of the realistic one in which you get rich painfully. But it doesn't have to be too painful. I can help you there, by giving you ways to avoid the pain and build the proper thinking to be successful. To the extent you have pain, it will only be from your own mind—since it certainly won't come from the steady march of stocks and real estate as they go ever higher. My favorite quote for the problem of mental pain is more than 400 years old.

> *"The mind is its own place, and in itself can make*
> *a Heaven of Hell, a Hell of Heaven."*
>
> —John Milton, *Paradise Lost*

You don't need to have been an English major to understand that Milton is saying it's all in our head or our perspective. That is what this book is for: to give you a new perspective on investing, one in which you give up trying to control the market and let it work for you. My goal is that you will see the market as heaven, not hell.

The overwhelming logic of buying quality assets and letting them appreciate immediately struck me as being right and true. Ever since I

read *Buffett, The Intelligent Investor,* and *One Up on Wall Street,*
I realized that much of what I had learned in my training was a load of
nonsense. The Buffett book was one of dozens of books on the greatest
mind in the history of stocks. Benjamin Graham, Buffett's mentor,
wrote *The Intelligent Investor* in the 1940s as a follow-up to his 1935
book *Security Analysis* with David Dodd. Peter Lynch wrote *One Up
on Wall Street,* which I believe is still the most accessible and practical
book that you can read. In the time it will take you to plan your next
vacation, you will have read three of the most worthwhile books on
investing from the three greatest minds in stock-market history.

These three people have had a profound (and profitable) effect
on me. *Mindful Money* cites concepts from these three liberally and
often, and for good reason: They have changed my economic destiny
and, more importantly, my family's welfare and the causes I care
deeply about. I will not try to teach you investment skills—there are
plenty of books for that, and I would start with the three experts I have
mentioned. There are many, many other investors who have used the
same approach, because it is *the only approach that works.* When I say
"works," I mean that it delivers "persistency of returns": a strategy that
works over time and through all economic conditions.

What works is simultaneously very easy and very hard. The easy
part is that you have to do very little work to succeed. The hard part
is that you must get out of your own way *mentally.* You are probably
a lot like me. You want to believe the easy story or the titillating story
instead of the hard, long and boring story that is true. You think the
wrong thoughts at times. Where do those thoughts come from? That
was the real question I wanted to answer for investors, because training
in selection of investments does you no good if you don't have the right
set of thoughts to execute your knowledge.

Ultimately, I want you to see through the endless stream of nonsense
that we have heard about investing, and I want you to avoid the stupid
mistakes I've made since buying my first stock over 35 years ago.

The Internet has created a vast wasteland of useless information in
addition to a new frontier of useful information. It is a blessing and a
curse. With that information, good or bad, comes the responsibility to
discern what is true and what is not. When it comes to money, the vast
majority of us will make many wrong choices. For evidence, you only

need look at the sad financial reality of those who should be saving and investing and do neither.

When the market goes up 300 points, no one ever describes it as volatile. But let it go down 300 points, and you will hear the word *volatile* all day long on CNBC and Bloomberg. It's a problem of human nature, so you need to be able to laugh and roll your eyes when you hear these things. The media is not there to help. News has become almost exclusively commentary.

This is not the book I originally set out to write. My initial concept was to expose the false data and misinformation we receive daily in our world of instant communication and the resulting fallacies and biases people exhibit in decision-making. Some of that remains, but I shifted my focus after coming across a website about Dr. Jeffrey Schwartz at UCLA, who had just published *You Are Not Your Brain*. I was intrigued by his research on the brain and its ability to change at any age, so I ordered the book and read it. I read it again and highlighted it. Everything seemed to make sense.

A couple of months later, I traveled to Westwood, California, to spend a couple of days with Dr. Schwartz, who was very generous with his time during our visit and in subsequent conversations. His knowledge and insight have been essential to me in understanding how people change and process information.

People are trapped in habits and patterns of thinking that are extremely difficult to change. The good news is that science has an answer. Platitudes from motivational and self-help books have helped people realize where they need to change, although they often boil down to thinking positively, being nicer to others, or showing more gratitude. They're long on advice, with little practical help on how to make these changes. In the past 20 years, discoveries about the brain are changing the way we think about *change*.

I believe that we investors—not investments—are the key ingredient to our success. We do not need to change or find new investment ideas. *We need to change ourselves to be successful.* I see investors continually sabotaging their long-term goals with bad decisions based on short-term events. *Mindful Money* will show you a way around that problem.

The book is divided into three sections:

SECTION 1 introduces the concepts and explains the problem of *investor* behavior being more important than *investment* behavior.

SECTION 2 dives into the process my firm has used successfully to help clients reach their goals of financial freedom. This is a step-by-step method that will help you choose the right advisors or use the right process.

SECTION 3 is where change can begin. This section is the key to making long-term changes that can help you become wealthy. I will describe and explain new studies about the human brain and how it changes. More important, I will lay out a proven formula to change the habits that keep you from being successful with your finances. This step is the key to change the number-one variable in your success: *your own behavior*. Mind you, this isn't psychobabble or New Age hocus-pocus. It's proven research, some of which has been around for more than six decades. It has been proven to work in real life. The ideas presented about changing habits and thought patterns are fast and effective.

If changing your investment approach is so simple, why doesn't everyone do it? Good question. Let's try an analogy: It wasn't until around 1920 that the first book was written on the concept of consuming fewer calories per day than we burned—it was brand-new science at that time. Since then, countless thousands of books have been published to tell us how to lose weight, even though it is now common knowledge that reduced-calorie diets work. How has that worked for us? Are we less overweight or more overweight with the knowledge we have?

The process of accumulating wealth is challenging, but far from impossible. Like losing weight and keeping it off, or changing any ingrained bad habit, you must be willing to make a change and take the steps. I believe all the information is here. So let's get started.

—Craig Verdi
February 2017

SECTION 1: THE PROBLEM

◆

Contrary to popular belief, the major part of an investor's return is not determined by asset allocation: i.e., what "basket" of stocks you are in. Nor is it determined by the overall performance of the stock market or real estate markets. The main predictor of return is the behavior of investors themselves. We don't see people with investment problems; we see investments with people problems.

While it's enticing to think there are strategies that can be deployed to make lots of money in the market reliably and quickly, in reality there are none. ***Investing in stocks is a get-rich-slow scheme.***

I realize "none" is a very small number. If I can get a few of you to agree, ignore the sales pitches and claims, and go about the real business of making money with stocks, I will have accomplished my mission.

In the first section, I throw out a challenge to our industry: Don't show us false returns. Don't show us hypothetical returns by using back-testing—feeding data into computers to find what *would have done well* over the last 10, 20, or 30 years—to produce a sales brochure. No real human could have invested in what you are looking at in many sales pieces created by financial salespeople.

Investors also need to be educated on what to avoid. Most con artists are easy to spot, because they operate outside a regulated environment. Their movements are opaque in an industry that is moving toward transparency. I will give a short history on how the infamous financial swindler Bernie Madoff and some others were able to succeed under the radar of regulators and why that happened.

I will spend very little time talking about individual investments, because my goal is to point you where to look and where not to look. Ridiculous promises are a constant of human history. They are just easier to produce convincingly in the age of the Internet and instant communication. The other side of that is that there is also an endless and ongoing amount of very valuable information.

The main thing to take away from section one is to be very sure of your sources and what you believe. The old saw "If it sounds too good to be true, it probably is" is very much in play. Yet, sometimes things that actually are true sound too good to be true. For instance, you will certainly be amazed at the amounts of money that patience would have made you in boring investments such as Wal-Mart or McDonald's. You may also be surprised by the results of compounding and the Rule of 72 (see Appendix 3) and of the power of it to grow wealth.

Ridiculous promises are a constant of human history.
They are just easier to produce convincingly in the age of the Internet and instant communication.

You may ask, if it is so easy, why doesn't everyone do it? The answer, you will see, is that patience is not easy at all—but it is absolutely necessary to the intelligent investor.

Magical Thinking

Magical thinking is a term I use throughout the book. In general, magical thinking is the attribution of *causal relationships* between actions and events that cannot be justified by reason and observation. Thousands of years ago, tribesman needed rain to survive. Nothing seemed to work, then one day the tribal priest danced. The clouds gave forth downpour of rain. Then, it happened again with enough regularity to convince the tribe that the dancing caused the rain.

Humans are pattern seekers. We try to make order out of randomness to make sense of the world. The term *magical thinking* refers to our attempt to make coherence out of incoherence, when there is none—and it's applicable to any type of superstition or fanciful thinking in regard to wealth planning.

It is your responsibility to filter out the nonsense. It is your money and your family's money, and it is up to you to use it for the great purposes in life and not squander it on some story you see on TV or the Internet.

Before you invest, you need trust. It can be found if you look in the right places. Although you'll never convince the conspiracy theorists, we have the most orderly and honest markets in the history of the world. There is no reason we can't all succeed in this type of environment. The foundation has been laid. Now we just need to get out of our own way.

CHAPTER 1

Why Can't I Accumulate Money?

"The market is the great allocator...
from the impatient to the patient."

—Warren Buffett

Why is it so difficult to accumulate wealth over time by investing in stocks or real estate? We have all seen the examples of what would have happened if you had put $100 per month away for 30 years in a particular investment, or what would have become of $100,000 if you bought a stock or property 20 years ago and you still owned it today. But why hasn't that happened for you? *Mindful Money* will answer that question. In fact, I believe we already know the answer. Much like getting in shape or losing weight, or developing intellectual or spiritual discipline, the answer lies in our own *volition*. The answer is in the mirror. *Mindful Money* will show you how to overcome the thoughts that sabotage your efforts to accumulate real wealth.

With investing, lack of information has never been the problem. In fact, today, we are bombarded by constant information, as well as its evil sidekicks: opinion and misinformation. The great investors are there for us to see. We just need to go do what really works and not what the guy on CNBC is selling. In the 1940s, Benjamin Graham laid out the keys to success in *The Intelligent Investor*. In the 1990s, Peter Lynch gave us plenty of information to act on with *One Up on Wall Street*. Jeremy Siegel gave us more than enough to work with in *Stocks for the Long-Run* in 1994, and has revised it several times—including a version after the recession of 2008 and beyond. Berkshire Hathaway's Warren Buffett and Charlie Munger have been a two-man traveling road show, with books, lectures, video, and all of the how-to we could ever need.

It is rarely the how-to that stops us from successful endeavors; it's usually discipline and patience. My experience in this business is that we don't see a lot of people with investment problems, we see investments with people problems. Buffett, in his commentary on the 1986 reprint of *The Intelligent Investor,* answers the question: "If it is so easy, why doesn't everyone do it?"

"I can only tell you that the secret has been out for 50 years, ever since Ben Graham and Dave Dodd wrote *Security Analysis*, yet I have seen no trend toward value investing in the 35 years that I've practiced it. There seems to be some perverse human characteristic that likes to make easy things difficult. The academic world, if anything, has actually backed away from the teaching of value investing over the last 30 years. It's likely to continue that way. Ships will sail around the world but the Flat Earth Society will flourish."

I started in the investment business at about the same time those words were spoken. They are just as true now—if not more so—than they were then. The quote is more than 30 years old, so now the so-called secret has been out for 80 years.*

We don't see many people with investment problems; we see investments with people problems.

We have the *know-how.* We know long-term investing in the right assets makes people wealthy, just as surely as exercise and diet mixed with discipline and determination produces weight loss. We already have more information than we can use. It is not the information or the facts that help us succeed in weight loss or long-term investing. The problem lies within us, in our brains. So, if you don't change the way you think, you won't help your portfolio or your waistline. It's simple and intuitive. What is not simple or intuitive, however, is the process we

---

*If you had invested $1,000 in Class A shares at the $19 price per share during Buffett's takeover in 1964, you would have owned 52 shares. At the closing price of BRK.A shares of $189,640 on Jan. 26, 2016, your 52 shares would have been worth $9,861,280, providing a theoretical 986,028% rate of return over a 52-year period. The S&P 500, on the other hand, increased by "only" about 2,300% over that time.

must go through to change our thinking. This book will show you how and give you the resources to continue to improve your thinking to act more effectively in your self-interest. These changes will also be in the best interest of those you love and care about, and probably for the rest of us as well.

There is a basic problem with the human brain: It is not wired for the long term. It is wired to react to save our skin in the short run. We are well prepared to get out of the way of an object, like a baseball or a speeding car. The problem lies with all the stress spent over getting out of the way of things that are coming at us *only in our minds.*

This quote by psychologist Daniel Gilbert introduces the concept:

"Our ability to duck that which is not yet coming is one of the brain's most stunning innovations, and we wouldn't have dental floss or 401(k) plans without it. But this innovation is in the early stages of development. The application that allows us to respond to visible baseballs is ancient and reliable, but the add-on utility that allows us to respond to threats that loom in an unseen future is still in beta testing."

Our brain is not too adept at long-term planning. There are great variations in our God-given abilities, from very good long-term planners to those who pretty much live each minute as it comes— but it is a skill you can improve.

Fear and Greed

Fear is the greatest reason we are not successful at investing. Legendary football coach Vince Lombardi once said, "Fatigue makes cowards of us all." There is nothing more fatiguing than watching your investments go down, day after day, month after month. The stress is sometimes too great. Even though we intellectually know we should stay put, we are not able to do it *emotionally.* So we sell, usually when the market is down. And when do we get back in? Only after the market has gone back up and we have confidence. The cycle repeats and we end up washing out the returns that history would have given us for free.

If you've been investing for some time, this is nothing new. You have heard it all before. You go to cash at the bottom of the market cycle and stay there for months or years. Then one night—at the third Christmas party in a row with people telling you how dumb you are for being in cash, and that their mutual funds have gone up 25% per year since you got out—you decide to get back in. Now you know where this is headed, don't you? It's old, painful ground, nothing new.

In the early years of my career, I made these mistakes too many times. I have lived through years of my own bad decisions and many years of good decisions. Good decisions work better. It was a slow, painful process and one that is unfortunately common in our business. Not all advisors are good at following their own advice— think of the physician who is overweight or smokes cigarettes. We often don't practice what we preach. Once I started living it, it became an obsession for me to teach this to my clients and to stick to my convictions.

There is good news. It's never too late to change. The need for smart investing doesn't magically stop when you hit 65 or 75. The average couple at age 62 has 30 more years of inflation ahead of them. Inflation is the second-biggest threat to your long-term investment success, after the fear and greed cycle. The fear and greed cycle never stops—it is how you react that matters. Having the ability to take advantage of values during the periods of great opportunity, which follow the capitulation phase of the market, will speed your success. *Capitulation* is when the last investors that are going to give up do give up. Now the market has everyone out who is getting out. Maximum opportunity lurks, but fear keeps us from doing the right thing. (*See figure 1.*)

We will talk much about the power of fear, because it is fear that creates the biggest obstacle to long-term investing success. It is said that the ***fear of loss is greater than the promise of gain***. While that's true, there is another thought in play that often trumps that: ***"I can't live with the idea that there may be a better, quicker, smarter, or more sophisticated way—that I am not doing."*** We can describe this fearful thought as "I should have."

Figure 1

Fear of loss is greater than the promise of gain…but there is another thought in play that often trumps that…

Avoiding the thought of "I should have" is acted out several ways. One way is by kicking yourself for not holding on to an investment that later went up, or not getting in on an investment that you "knew was going up." There are a few more variations, but these two cover many of them. This involves two errors. One is a common cognitive thinking error, the other a common logical fallacy. The cognitive thinking error is "should statements." Those make no sense, since you are not omniscient. No matter how many times you think this painful thought, it does not advance you toward your goal.

The logical fallacy involved is hindsight bias. For such occasions, I keep a copy of the *Wall Street Journal* from 10 years ago in my desk. When a client starts saying things like "I should have invested in XYZ stock," I threaten to pull out that *Wall Street Journal* and a box of Kleenex so we can go on a crying jag, picking out the things we could have invested in (in hindsight) and made a fortune on. This is serious wrong thinking. It deludes us into thinking we could have known how things would have turned out. Of course we could not, and more importantly, don't need to. We simply must act today, wherever we are, and invest for the long run with the best information we now have.

We are haunted by the thought that there may be or must be a better, quicker, smarter, or more sophisticated way that is different from what we are doing. The pain of "I should have" is too great.

A number of cognitive thinking errors and logical fallacies keep you from your financial goals. Using *Mindful Money* principles, we will learn to avoid these and other thinking errors that keep us from being accumulators of wealth.

When I was new in the business, I believed that once clients had a lot of money and reached a certain age—say, 80—they would become less concerned about money problems and be able to focus on grandchildren, philosophy, and relaxation. After all, they had created plenty of assets to take care of their major needs. For the most part, unfortunately, this just has not been the case. In fact, some people get more concerned about money as they age, which is truly sad. Let's make sure that doesn't happen to you. I have had clients for decades, and have watched the ones that I have helped be relaxed and confident and the ones that can't seem to get there. Their minds are consumed with world affairs, politics, taxes, social issues, and just about anything that is contrary to the image of peaceful, wise, and happy grandparents that we all wish we had.

There are commonsense reasons why you have to be in stocks or some kind of equity ownership to make real money. "The rich get richer" is true; they are the holders of equity. They have all the real stuff. The holders of equity get rich. These people are the owners. In contrast, we are loaners if we have money in banks or bonds. The vast majority of wealth is built slowly over time by the patient holding of good assets.

Entertainers, inventors, professional athletes, and corporate executives are the exceptions. They have the ability to make so much so fast that they don't necessarily have to own investments. Odds are, we aren't going to be one of them. And even if you are, you have heard about too many professional athletes who just couldn't manage their money once they had it. This book is even more important if you have a large sum of money coming.

So how do we proceed with confidence? Can you, for once, be that person who has been successful in the market? There is no need to be exceptional in the market; you only need to *participate* in the returns over time and reinvest distributions. To do this, you must have the right mindset. People who invest poorly often aren't hindered by what they invested in, but when they got in and when they got out. We are wired with an overwhelming urge to get out at the bottom and in at the top. The average investor is great at extrapolating all the wrong thoughts into the future. Here is the dismal state of what people investing *get* vs. what they were invested in *got*:

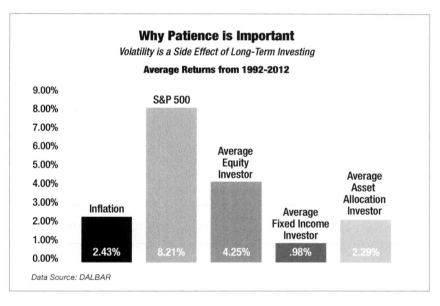

What the chart above reveals is the difference between what the market has *provided* compared to what the average investor has *collected*. Every year, Dalbar publishes this running 20-year record of investor returns vs. market returns. How does the average investor make *less than half* the return of the actual market? There is only one reason: It is the behavior of the investors that determine return. A small percentage of investors do better than the markets. Investors seem to be focused on trying to be part of *that small percentage* instead of first concentrating on matching or coming close to matching the market returns.

What's behind the huge disconnect between what the market provides and what we collect? The answer is fear. Fear causes us to act in ways that are not in our best interests.

The natural laws of investing have already been set, so we need to learn to comply. We must not fight gravity, we must not fight history, and we must not fight reality. Savvy investors already understand this. They have given up on superstition. They realize dread is not a strategy. They bet on history, collecting the instructions history has given them. In doing so, they become wealthy.

What has worked and is proven. I am a strong believer that value investing is the basis for success in the market. Forbes has a workable definition: "An investing theory that suggests that markets systematically undervalue companies with high cash flow but large book values and stable businesses. Investors following this theory tend to screen stocks based on financial statement data, invest for the long term and do not change investments very often. They invest in stocks with a low price-to-earnings ratio (P/E), high dividend yield, low price-to-book value (P/B), and low price-to-sales ratio (P/S)." I would add that a company's ability to raise dividends over time is also a key factor.

The main point is that in the long run, the price of a stock is tied to earnings of the company and the growth of those earnings. All else is temporary and illusory and, in my experience, cannot be sustained over long periods of time. There are always stories of people getting rich quickly. If you want to build solid, sure wealth, you will most likely be a *long-term value investor*.

I realize that you may say, "I know this guy that made millions off of (fill in the blank), and he used the Such-and-Such Method." I will demonstrate, after exhaustive research, that:

There is no evidence that persistency of returns can be demonstrated over long periods (25 years or more) by using methods such as technical analysis (charts), options, short selling, day trading or active trading, or any market-timing schemes of any kind. These funds would have to have a verifiable, audited track record that is superior to those track records of well-known value investors. These funds must

be investable (open) to the general public, including high-net-worth investors and institutions.

This is the thesis as posed to more than 50 sources. I am sure I will get a lot of replies about this or that manager produced this or that return. Before you email me, make sure they are verifiable by empirical evidence, and are publicly discernable and audited by generally accepted accounting principles.

Conclusion

No options are available that have produced real-world empirical evidence for persistency of returns that beat the proven track records of well-known value investors as defined above.

My research included hundreds of iterations of "best track record for funds" before soliciting feedback from investment research departments at major mutual-fund companies and brokerage houses. The question has been emailed to or we have spoken to more than 50 research departments to try to verify this conclusion. While there may be some outliers that were overlooked, they are extremely rare or nonexistent. People persist in believing what they want to hear. What they usually want to hear is that there is indeed a better, quicker, smarter, or more sophisticated way that is different from what they are doing.

This does not make me popular with the research departments at mutual-fund companies or brokerage firms. Most, but not all, believe that they have some special way of beating the market other than the proven way. Even billionaires and PhDs are not remotely immune to this egregious form of magical thinking. Nonetheless, not one of the analysts I spoke with, without exception, could produce a long-term track record of an actual fund that is investable by the public—including foundations, institutions, or billionaires—that can replicate what has been accomplished by Buffett and other long-term investors over the past three decades.

I have been sent many nebulous "track records." A lot of these records include periods in which the fund was not available or had other questionable data. The returns need to be verified. Anyone can show you a page of hypothetical or back-tested returns. The records need to be audited by a reliable independent source and reported numbers of an investment company that is regulated under the Investment Act of 1940 or other similar entity, or be self-reporting with transparent data.

You don't have to be Buffett or be as patient as Buffett to succeed. You just need to collect on what history will give you.

Why have all these methods been invented and studied at top business schools, if they don't work? The theory is that all this investment complexity did not come about solely from marketing departments or because it was proven. I have concluded:

Complexity in financial markets has come about, for the most part, by the need for people to "self-medicate" with complicated strategies, such as technical analysis, active trading and derivatives. The thought of holding quality assets and doing nothing, is just too hard for most people to do. They must be moving, they must feel they are in control. They continue to use strange and unproven strategies to "self-medicate" the pain of exercising patience.

I will lay out the evidence as we move forward. *Self-medicating*, as I have called it, is played out in a desperate attempt to have control over that which we don't. I am not talking about scams and get-rich-quick schemes, which are dangerous but easily avoidable. I am referring to techniques taught at the PhD level at the best universities in the world. The amazing thing about them? They simply don't work. I know that is a hard pill to swallow. As I go through the book, I will argue that even as proven strategies are out there, *our need to be "doing something" has sabotaged us all the way along.*

Chapter 1 Takeaways:

1. Investors underperform *investments*.

2. There is no lack of information. We can clearly see what has worked and what has not worked.

3. Thinking of dangers that never happen will put you on the wrong path and waste time and energy.

4. The fear and greed cycle is one of the reasons we have opportunity.

5. There is no need to be exceptional at investing in stocks. You merely need to participate in market growth to succeed.

6. The secret has been out for 80 years.

7. Investments are not complex because they need to be; they are complex because investors think they need to be *"doing something."* All of these crazy strategies cost time and money, and are only there in a desperate attempt to avoid fear.

8. Fear is the most powerful emotion to overcome in investing.

9. After exhaustive research, I can only conclude that there are no existing strategies that will beat long-term, buy-and-hold value investing.

Mindful Money Questions:

1. Can you think of a stock that you didn't buy and later told yourself: "I knew I should have purchased that stock"?

2. Have you ever waited for "just the right time" to get in the market— and never found the right time?

3. Have you ever owned a stock for 20 years that paid increasing dividends?

CHAPTER 2

You Only Have Two Choices

"Dread is not a strategy."

—Nick Murray, author of *Simple Wealth, Inevitable Wealth*

*"You can't reason someone out of something
they weren't reasoned into in the first place."*

—Anonymous

The problem with investing successfully is all in your head. That may not make you happy, but it should. If you knew for sure a painful physical symptom was due to your thoughts, you could get instant relief… if you knew how to change your brain to stop the symptoms.

Alas, no one can offer proof or convince you of anything you don't want to believe. Many patients with a dreaded symptom will go from doctor to doctor, looking for the answer they are looking for. Investors do exactly the same thing. They move from advisor to advisor or strategy to strategy, until one tells them something they want to hear. Before long, someone will.

What they want to hear is always the same thing: "We can get you out of the market before it goes down, and get you back in before it goes up," or some version of that statement. It won't take more than a few visits to the local broker before you hear those blessed words. That's when the real trouble begins, because it is a lie. The person may not be conscious that the statement is false, but it is a lie nonetheless. Someone has convinced the advisor they can do the impossible and, hoping against hope that he has found the Holy Grail, they retell the lie to clients.

At our firm, we see these investors quite often. The only thing that will help is to change their thinking, as with our example of a physical pain that's all in your head. Some doctors may offer suggestions that work as a placebo and give temporary relief, and others may be reluctant to point out that the patient's own thoughts are at the root of the problem. It is really tough medicine. The patient doesn't like to hear it. Many investors don't want to hear the cure either.

I'm not interested in placebos, and I want to show you the cure: accepting the long, hard grind and discipline that value investing represents.

At the risk of oversimplifying, there are basically two approaches to investing:

1. Buy great companies and wait.
2. Everything else.

My position is that approach number 2 will fail 99% of the time. You could hit it rich with a penny stock or unheard-of invention, but you might also win Powerball or hit the $3 million jackpot at the progressive slot machines in Las Vegas. You could also win "American Idol" or "America's Got Talent." While we're dreaming, you could also be Hollywood's next box-office superstar.

So let's look at number 1, using Wal-Mart as an example of a successful company. (Note: I am not recommending Wal-Mart as an investment here. You should always hold a basket of stocks, since they don't all work out this well.) The following chart compares Wal-Mart against the overall stock market as measured by the S&P 500 index. The chart is pretty self-explanatory. You would have enjoyed over 100,000% return on your money in 30 years, compared to about a 2,500% return on the S&P. Outside of the Walton family, which owns Wal-Mart, how many individual or fund investors do you think collected on that entire return? My guess is very few.

Wal-Mart Stores, Inc. Common Stock vs. S&P 500

■ WMT   ▨ S&P 500

Data Source: Yahoo!

The purpose here is to offer "proof" that there are reliable time-tested methods that will help you accumulate true wealth. I put *proof* in quotes just because truth, even when presented well, does not always help get people to believe it. Proof and facts don't usually motivate people to take action. They must have an expectation of good things happening as a result of investing.

A quick story to explain the futility of preaching proof. I am a longtime fan of financial industry writer Nick Murray, quoted at the top of this chapter. He tells a story in which you enter an elevator in New York City to find a man in the fetal position sucking on his thumb. When you inquire as to his situation, he explains that he is deathly afraid that the elevator will fall and he will plunge to his death. You, an engineer for the city, just happen to have a briefcase full of material on this very subject. You have charts, graphs, and statistics on the rate of elevator accidents in New York since elevators were first installed. You whip out your proof to help this poor man. You show him that in over a billion trips in an elevator, no one has died in a fall! Now you have helped the man—he'll feel much better and get up off the floor to thank you, right? No, he doesn't. He continues to lie there sobbing. The facts you present have no effect on him. You are of no help to him—and may have even made him worse. Why? He may conclude that you just increased his odds of dying because now the elevator is due to fall!

Moral of the story: Don't be the Elevator Guy.

So, despite my own advice to the contrary, I will try to add some proof to your investment expectations. I will also try to give you a different outlook on investing than you have previously had. You must have the correct outlook on what your rewards will be for what you give up. You will give up money to invest, but the real costs will be paid emotionally if you are not convinced of the results. The emotional pain of a fluctuating market can be anywhere from zero to unbearable. This is all determined by your thoughts. If you are fearful, you will pay a high price. *If you are fearless, you will pay nothing.*

Long-term value investing in stocks and real estate starts with a very simple premise. You must *believe* in this statement to be successful at investing, and if you don't believe it, you will never get the results you desire. The premise is this:

Quality equity assets increase in value over long periods of time.

Almost 100% of equity assets are made up of two broad asset classes: 1) ownership of companies and 2) real estate. You can own your own company directly or invest in shares of companies that will allow you to do it. You can own real estate directly or buy it in mutual funds or real estate investment trusts (REITs). Commodities such as metals, precious metals, wheat, and corn are not equity. They do not generally stay ahead of inflation.

If you take a look at the Forbes 400 list of the richest people in the United States, you will see that, without exception, billionaires are created in only two ways: ownership of stock or real estate. Some of these people got rich on their own—so-called *new money*—but the vast majority have received it, passed down through several generations. What is passed down? Quality equity assets. Not one of them got to be billionaires by handing down a trainload of metal or grain for several generations. That doesn't create wealth. In many cases, commodities deplete wealth.

If you are asking, "Who wouldn't believe that?" you are a candidate for investing successfully. If you don't agree or are skeptical, let me add some definitions. First, I would say *a long period* is a minimum of 15 years, and 20 or 25 years is an even more appropriate standard. Think of investing in decades—not years, months, or, even worse, days. Second, when I say, "Quality assets will appreciate in value," I am asking you to imagine such things as:

- Your residence will be worth more in 20 years than it is now.
- Companies such as Costco, Boeing, Starbucks, and Johnson & Johnson will be selling more products in 20 years than they are today, and will be earning and paying out more money to shareholders.

Things get more expensive. Good companies grow. Well-located real estate becomes more valuable. Rents go up. You have to know that when you begin to invest, or *why would you ever begin?* We are not speculating on Ecuadorian silver-mining land or biotech startup companies. A long-term value investor chooses assets not to make a killing, but to be confident in the long-term growth prospects of these assets. He chooses to own enough of them so that most of them will succeed. He doesn't put all his eggs in one basket, but focuses instead on choosing good baskets. He invests, he does not speculate. Of course, I'm not the only one with that opinion:

Claims of "proprietary trading programs" pop up in several investment scams each year. It's a powerful pitch, the idea that the person who has your money knows something that other traders don't and is willing to let you be the beneficiary of his or her knowledge and skill. But if he or she has really cracked the code, really knows how to reap guaranteed profits, why would they need your money? Why the hassles of monthly statements and possible SEC investigations? The answer is always, always, that there is no "proprietary program." Vigilant investors consider that term a flashing warning sign and never go near any investment that claims it.
—The U.S. Securities and Exchange Commission

Be an owner not a loaner. None of the Forbes 400 people got rich by buying and holding bonds.

For your long-term goals, you should be the owner of the equity. The owner—the person with the equity—takes the risks, but owns the asset. The loaner lends money to the owner in the form of bank deposit or bonds. You want to be the owner. They are the people that get all the nice stuff. These are the people who don't agonize over compact vs. midsize at the car-rental counter. Be the owner.

Chapter 2 Takeaways:

1. What is an equity asset? Is there something you own now that has a history of appreciation? Maybe your residence or business? Almost all of the equity in the world is made up of corporations and real estate. You really don't have a third choice.

2. Commodities such as wheat and silver will never help you achieve wealth. The inflation-adjusted price of wheat is one-half of what it was in 1900.

3. There are only two basic investment strategies: 1. Hold on to quality shares over the long haul, and let the companies grow. 2. Everything else.

4. Quality equity assets, such as well-located real estate and quality companies get more valuable over time. You must believe that—or why would you ever invest?

5. When you buy CDs, bonds, or other non-equity investments, you are loaning your money out so those that borrow can own more equity and make more money than you. Be an owner, not a loaner.

6. Don't be the Elevator Guy.

7. This time is not different.

8. Investing in stocks is a get-rich-slow scheme.

Mindful Money Questions:

1. Are you a loaner or an owner?

2. What is your reward from long-term investing? You need to know the reward, because there is a cost. The first cost is your money. The biggest cost is the emotional cost you will pay if you are not ready for fluctuation.

3. Can you resist the temptation of hearing 20 gold commercials in one day?

4. Have you ever turned on the financial news and thought, "This time it's different"? Don't do that!

CHAPTER 3

Equity Assets vs. Debt

"Inflation is as violent as a mugger, as frightening as an armed robber, and as deadly as a hit man."

—President Ronald Reagan

Let's imagine an investment you made in 1980. You invested $160,000 in the investment. Today, it is worth $490,000. Assume you can sell it and pay a low tax rate of 20%, including state and federal taxes. Your gain is $330,000. Your taxes owed are $66,000. Your net gain is $264,000.

But…was it a good investment?

In fact it, was a lousy investment. Your return (the increase) in this example shows the inflation tied to a first-class postage stamp. Stamps were 16 cents in 1980 and are today 49 cents. That is an average compound increase of 3.8%. After taxes, your return is around 3%, a figure that would put you behind in your quest for wealth. Inflation took all of the money you thought you'd made. But, hey—at least you kept up with inflation. If you had it buried in the backyard you would have pulled out dollars that were worth about *34 cents.*

Our firm uses three common metrics to look at inflation. One is postage stamps. The others are the changes in home prices and teacher's salaries. These are fairly reliable real-world examples of inflation and how it directly impacts everything you buy. If your salary is $50,000 per year, it will be worth roughly $25,000 per year in 20 years at a 3% inflation rate. In effect, you must double your salary every 20 years or cut your spending in half.

If you insist on accumulating money in debt assets like CDs or bonds, you will never actually be invested and you will never create wealth.

***If you insist on accumulating money in debt assets
such as CDs or bonds, you will never actually be invested
and you will never create wealth.***

For a moment, imagine a world without inflation: Everything stays the same price forever. In this world you save money by stuffing money in your mattress monthly. If your income is $5,000 a month and you live on $4,000 a month, you will save $1,000 a month (20% of your income) in the mattress.

After 20 years of saving, you have $240,000, and now it's time to retire. You still need $4,000 a month to live on—which means you have exactly 80 months until you are broke. This is the same decision you make when you invest in bonds or bank deposits. You are going into the game knowing you will lose ground.

In a world with or without inflation, you still need to own equity assets. In the imaginary no-inflation world, real estate could still increase due to increasing demand and diminishing supply. Stock holdings could still increase in value by growing sales and profits and increasing dividends. Either way, you have to be an owner not a loaner.

How Do Stocks "Work"?

Why do good companies increase in value in the long run? The short answer is by increasing the sales, earnings, growth, and distributions/dividends of the company. Let's look at a very simple company you have a chance to invest in. Imagine that a young entrepreneur, Marcus, decides to open a hotdog stand on the corner of the street.

- The total cost of the business is $1,000.
- There are 100 shares available at $10 per share.
- You are offered 10 shares for a total investment of $100.
- You own exactly 10% of the business. You don't have to work, buy hot dogs, cook, collect money, pay sales tax, or do any of the other chores.
- Sales are $500 per year. Profits are $200.

- Next year, sales are expected to be $600, with $240 in profits.
- 25 cents per share is paid each year in dividends.

That gives us some good information that we can use to decide if we want to own this equity asset.

- The market cap is $1,000. Market cap is simply number of shares times the price per share, or 100*$10.
- The P/E ratio of the stock is 5. This is just the price per share divided by the profit per share, or $10/$2.
- The forward P/E ratio is 4.2. That's the current price divided by future profit estimates, or $10/$2.40.
- The P/S ratio is 2. The calculation is the price of the company divided by its sales, or $1000/$500.
- The dividend yield is 2.5%, which is $0.25/$10.
- You are an insider, because you own 10% of the company, while Marcus owns 90%.

Is this a good investment for the long term? If Marcus is successful for decades to come, this might be a *fantastic* investment. The first year, you made $2.50 in dividends and your shares produced $20 in earnings. You do not directly receive the earnings. When you run the numbers, though, you calculate that the shares may now be worth $12 per share, due to the 20% in increased profits.

The shares you own are available for you to sell back to Marcus or any other investor. For the sake of argument, let's say offers for your shares are listed daily in the media. You have several offers to buy your shares for $10–11.50. You say no. Each time a person makes an offer, the media lists the price of the shares at that price, and because that is the amount a willing buyer would offer you. Later, you are offered $14 per share. You also say no. Then, someone offers you $5, and no one else offers you any more for several months. The price in the media is now listed as $5, since that has been the price for the last several offers.

No one is willing to pay more than $5 for an extended period. You think your shares are worth $12, but you start to wonder if there is something other investors know that you don't. Thoughts begin to race through your head:

- Maybe Marcus has a criminal record that you're not aware of.
- Maybe his hotdogs contain cheap ingredients he is lying about.
- Maybe he is cooking the books, and not selling as many hot dogs as he says.

In this case, you happen to know for certain that all of that is false. There are no good or apparent reasons your shares are so cheap. What could you do?

1. Panic. You feel that there must be something wrong that you don't know (even though you are secure in your knowledge of the business) and sell your shares for $5.

2. Hold your shares and collect the dividends until better offers come in. By the way, your yield as reported in the media is now 5%. That is $0.25/$5. So while your yield is higher, the total value of your shares is now only $50.

3. Call Marcus and see if he wants to sell you more shares at the market price of $5.00.

Because of your knowledge of the business, the obvious thing would be to try to purchase more shares. You may or may not have the money available to buy more shares. Why would you not do the obvious and buy additional shares that you deem to be underpriced? There is only one reason: fear. You are upset, confused, and worried that the market offers of $5 must represent a basic weakness in the company, the economy, or world affairs. That is all the information about this saga of your investment into the hotdog stand industry, but it's precisely how public companies work.

Welcome to the world of stock investing.

The Mysterious Mechanism that Prices Your Stocks

Benjamin Graham called the imaginary entity that sets daily prices "Mr. Market." He described Mr. Market as a manic-depressive individual who really didn't know anything other than the emotions he was having at the time. Buffett likens the pricing mechanism to a crazy neighbor who yells out offers for your house randomly over the fence each day. In other words, it doesn't make a lot of sense, and there is no connection between the mechanism and the actual price of one share of a company.

If your shares are priced too high by Mr. Market, you shouldn't think that you are rich any more than you should think you are poor if his psychosis compels him to offer a low amount. This mechanism is constantly pricing shares at random prices. Prices react to news and earnings, etc., but never in a straight line. The actual value of your shares, as measured by popularly used metrics, is almost always at least slightly different than the market is offering you for your shares.

So what should you do? My advice is to disregard the market price at all times. Have a good idea of what your shares are worth. Over time, the shares will increase in value as earnings, dividends, and book value increase. It really is that simple. Sometimes it takes years for the disconnect between price and value to get resolved, but it always will. Your shares will go up eventually.

> *Buffett likens the pricing mechanism to a crazy neighbor who yells out offers for your house randomly over the fence each day.*

If you are under 80 years old, the worst market correction in your life happened in 2008–09, and it was a doozy. I believe most people assume that since their shares went way down that the actual value or utility of the company also decreased. In some cases, that was true. But in the great majority, there was no reason for the shares to go down other than the collective psychology of individual and institutional investors.

If you were prepared—and not fearful—2009 became a once-in-a-lifetime opportunity to pick up great companies at ridiculously low prices.

What about Bonds?

"Don't you think I should have a certain percentage in bonds?
Everything I read says that I should have 20–50% of my money in
bonds." I hear these things all the time. And there have been good
times to buy bonds. As I'm writing this, the yield on the 10-year Federal
Treasury bond is at 2.5%. The yield has historically been much higher.
When has it been this low before? Never. What about during the Great
Depression? Or 100 years ago? Nope, not even then. See the chart on
page 31 to get an idea of just how remarkable this time in history is.
We have been in 32-year bull market for bonds. No one thinks they can
crash, but they can and will.

How do they crash? As I'll explain in more detail in a moment, they
do so by interest rates spiking rapidly higher. The unusually low rates
and 30-plus years of steadily dropping rates have brought us to this.
(Note: By the time you read this, the situation may have changed, but
the concepts are the same.)

Even my hero Benjamin Graham said that investors should always
keep some of their money in bonds, and when stocks rise they should
take profits and put them in bonds. When he gave that advice, however,
the yield on 10-year Treasuries was 3–5%. If you could get those types
of rates now, I might recommend the same approach. He also wrote that
the main reason for doing this was to *keep investors occupied*, give them
something to do to take their minds off of the stock market! I like that
advice. But with rates this low, it is not only bad advice, it could be risky.

I have believed rates will go higher from some time, but I don't
concern myself with it, since I am not in bonds. Can bonds crash? Yes,
they can! Are they safe? Let's look briefly on how bonds work. First of
all bonds are debt. When governments and companies want to borrow
money, they issue bonds. You give them money, they pay you interest.
So when you hear about the "debt portion" of a portfolio, it is referring
to bonds. Bonds are also called *fixed income*, which is a more widely
used term and sounds better than debt.

Here's a quick Q&A on bonds and how they work:

Q: What are bonds?
A: Bonds are just loans. The issuer may be a government or another entity like a corporation. You give them money; they pay you a fixed interest rate. Bonds are usually $1,000 each. For now we will assume they all are $1,000. If you buy a 10-year bond today with a yield (also known as a coupon) of 2%, you will get paid $20 per year for the next 10 years. At the end of the 10 years, you get your money back. It's that easy.

Q: What if I don't want to wait 10 years? Say I sell in 5 years?
A: You can cash out in five years.

Q: How much will I get if I cash out before the 10 years are up?
A: Good question. It depends on what interest rates are when you cash out.

Q: What if rates are higher when I cash out?
A: This part is counterintuitive. Many people would guess that rates going up would be good, but that's not the case. Why? Because your bond pays 2%. If the bonds five years in the future pay new investors 4%, who wants your bond? No one, because they can get new ones at 4%.

Q: How do I cash out?
A: You cash out to the highest bidder. Since that bidder can now buy a 4% bond, you need to "sweeten the pot" and offer your $1,000 bond at a *discount*—perhaps $900.

Q: What if rates are lower when I cash out?
A: Let's say that rates have fallen to 1%. Now who wants your 2% bond? Everyone, because they can only get 1% on the new ones. This is great— you can ask for a *premium* price for your bond! Since everyone else has to buy new bonds at 1% yield and you are holding one that pays twice as much, you are in the money! You may get, for instance, $1,100.

Q: What if it's longer or shorter than 10 years?
A: Hopefully your instincts will say, "Well, if I have to wait 20 or 30 years to get my money back, that will make the bond much more attractive when rates fall (because I have a higher yield)." When rates go

up, I will be stuck for longer at the lower rate, so who wants my bond if rates go up? Nobody. If rates go up, you lose.

Q: How much could I lose?

A: It is hard to say, since bonds are driven by buyers and sellers. Let's use a different example. Say I put $100,000 this morning into a 30-year bond with a 3.5% yield. This afternoon, rates go up to 7%. That would probably never happen, but if it did, the fair price of your bonds would be $50,000. And you're still stuck for 30 years at the lower rate. Despite bonds having a reputation of safety, there can be considerable risk, and what do you get in return? A lousy 3.5%. No ownership, just 30 years of loaner-ship.

Q: Should I invest in bonds?

A: You should think about putting money in bonds at times. If you need income from the bonds, you may consider individual bonds. I would recommend you buy a good income bond mutual fund or exchange traded fund (ETF), which is a much easier and better way to access bonds. The time to buy bonds is when the yield on the bonds is *higher than the rate of inflation*. Our firm looks at the 10-year Treasury as a barometer of bond rates. If the yield is above the long-term rate of inflation, I may be a buyer. (Note: As of the time of this book's publication, I am almost 100% out of bonds in my personal portfolio and clients have very little in bond holdings.)

Q: Do bonds compound and reinvest like stocks and funds and put the Rule of 72 to work?

A: No. This is a major weakness of individual bonds unless you are going to spend the interest anyway. If bond yields are high, they may be a good way to generate income.

Again, bonds have been in a bull market (falling interest rates) for as long as most of us can remember. We are not only at astoundingly low bond yields, but are lower than we have ever been in history. The chart on the next page shows the yield on the 10-year Treasury going back to 1872.

Date	10 Year Rate Value	Date	10 Year Rate Value	Date	10 Year Rate Value	Date	10 Year Rate Value
4/6/2015	1.92%	1/1/1975	7.50%	1/1/1934	3.12%	1/1/1893	3.75%
1/1/2015	1.88%	1/1/1974	6.99%	1/1/1933	3.31%	1/1/1892	3.60%
1/1/2014	2.86%	1/1/1973	6.46%	1/1/1932	3.68%	1/1/1891	3.62%
1/1/2013	1.91%	1/1/1972	5.95%	1/1/1931	3.34%	1/1/1890	3.42%
1/1/2012	1.97%	1/1/1971	6.24%	1/1/1930	3.29%	1/1/1889	3.45%
1/1/2011	3.39%	1/1/1970	7.79%	1/1/1929	3.60%	1/1/1889	3.45%
1/1/2010	3.73%	1/1/1969	6.04%	1/1/1928	3.33%	1/1/1888	3.67%
1/1/2009	2.52%	1/1/1968	5.53%	1/1/1927	3.34%	1/1/1887	3.52%
1/1/2008	3.74%	1/1/1967	4.58%	1/1/1926	3.68%	1/1/1886	3.37%
1/1/2007	4.76%	1/1/1966	4.61%	1/1/1925	3.86%	1/1/1885	3.52%
1/1/2006	4.42%	1/1/1965	4.19%	1/1/1924	4.06%	1/1/1884	3.62%
1/1/2005	4.22%	1/1/1964	4.17%	1/1/1923	4.36%	1/1/1883	3.63%
1/1/2004	4.15%	1/1/1963	3.83%	1/1/1922	4.30%	1/1/1882	3.62%
1/1/2003	4.05%	1/1/1962	4.08%	1/1/1921	5.09%	1/1/1881	3.70%
1/1/2002	5.04%	1/1/1961	3.84%	1/1/1920	4.97%	1/1/1880	4.02%
1/1/2001	5.16%	1/1/1960	4.72%	1/1/1919	4.50%	1/1/1879	4.22%
1/1/2000	6.66%	1/1/1959	4.02%	1/1/1918	4.57%	1/1/1878	4.34%
1/1/1999	4.72%	1/1/1958	3.09%	1/1/1917	4.23%	1/1/1877	4.45%
1/1/1998	5.54%	1/1/1957	3.46%	1/1/1916	4.05%	1/1/1876	4.59%
1/1/1997	6.58%	1/1/1956	2.90%	1/1/1915	4.24%	1/1/1875	5.07%
1/1/1996	5.65%	1/1/1955	2.61%	1/1/1914	4.16%	1/1/1874	5.47%
1/1/1995	7.78%	1/1/1954	2.48%	1/1/1913	4.45%	1/1/1873	5.58%
1/1/1994	5.75%	1/1/1953	2.83%	1/1/1912	4.01%	1/1/1872	5.36%
1/1/1993	6.60%	1/1/1952	2.68%	1/1/1911	3.98%		
1/1/1992	7.03%	1/1/1951	2.57%	1/1/1910	3.91%		
1/1/1991	8.09%	1/1/1950	2.32%	1/1/1909	3.76%		
1/1/1990	8.21%	1/1/1949	2.31%	1/1/1908	3.87%		
1/1/1989	9.09%	1/1/1948	2.44%	1/1/1907	3.67%		
1/1/1988	8.67%	1/1/1947	2.25%	1/1/1906	3.43%		
1/1/1987	7.08%	1/1/1946	2.19%	1/1/1905	3.48%		
1/1/1986	9.19%	1/1/1945	2.37%	1/1/1904	3.40%		
1/1/1985	11.38%	1/1/1944	2.48%	1/1/1903	3.30%		
1/1/1984	11.67%	1/1/1943	2.47%	1/1/1902	3.18%		
1/1/1983	10.46%	1/1/1942	2.46%	1/1/1901	3.10%		
1/1/1982	14.59%	1/1/1941	1.95%	1/1/1900	3.15%		
1/1/1981	12.57%	1/1/1940	2.21%	1/1/1899	3.10%		
1/1/1980	10.80%	1/1/1939	2.36%	1/1/1898	3.35%		
1/1/1979	9.10%	1/1/1938	2.56%	1/1/1897	3.40%		
1/1/1978	7.96%	1/1/1937	2.68%	1/1/1896	3.60%		
1/1/1977	7.21%	1/1/1936	2.65%	1/1/1895	3.46%		
1/1/1976	7.74%	1/1/1935	2.79%	1/1/1894	3.70%		

A Note on Commodities

Many people confuse commodities such as gold, silver, and copper as equity assets. They are not! Contrary to what the sellers are pitching, metals, crops, lumber, or almost any commodity has never kept up with inflation. There are times when certain commodities become very cheap, such as steel is today. We have steel coming out of our ears. It is cheaper than cabbage. There will be a time when it bounces back and money will be made, but it's still not a good bet to appreciate against inflation over long periods. My advice is to never invest in commodities.

Here's why: Investing in commodities is speculation. You have purchased a lump of something. The lump produces nothing. There are no dividends, no interest, and no earnings. You need to hope that when you sell it, another person is willing to give you a higher price. This is referred to as the "greater-fool theory" of investing, because you have to wait for someone more foolish, greedy, or misinformed to buy your lump. It may work, on occasion, in the short run, or if you get lucky. But I don't believe it has any place in a long-term investment plan alongside value stocks. Don't just take my word for it—here are some illustrations:

Wheat: Wheat sold for about $200 per ton 100 years ago. Today, it is about $500 per ton. That is an annual increase of 1.8%. There were spikes where speculators may have made money, but there were decades where it never moved. As I mentioned earlier, adjusted for inflation, *wheat is about half of the price it was 100 years ago.*

Gold: Gold was about $20 per ounce in 1850. Today, it is about $1,200 per ounce. That is an annual rate of return of about 2.5%. Most of that gain came after the gold standard was nixed by Nixon in 1971. It was being held by the government at the time at $35 per ounce. By 1980, the price hit $615. So, some speculators made a lot of money in less than a decade—but if you bought gold in 1980, you would have waited until 2007 to get back to even! Twenty-seven years with no dividends, no interest, and the cost of storing and insuring your lump of gold made it even more painful. Since 2007, we have experienced another increase to

$1,200, not quite doubling your money in eight years. That is a 9% rate of return, and you have to really cherry-pick to find the periods when you would have made money.

Investing in commodities is speculation. You have purchased a lump of something. The lump produces nothing. There are no dividends, no interest, and no earnings.

That is my honest take on commodities. There are numerous people online or elsewhere who will tell you they have figured out the secret to trading commodities *futures*. When you find them, could you please send me the actual, audited returns to a real investor, net of fees? The returns are dismal, and your lump is still a lump.

Two more things before I let the commodities issue rest. First, let's recall the Forbes 400 list of the 400 richest individuals in the world. In the top 10, the individuals listed have all made their money from a company stock, four of them from Wal-Mart. If we look at the top 400, there are three ways people got there. The first way is to invent something or be a founder of a fast-growing company. Mark Zuckerberg, founder of Facebook, is #20. The second way is to own stocks over long periods, usually handed down over a generation or two. In addition to the six Wal-Mart names, Microsoft, Intel, Apple, and others have multiple early stockholders who held on to their shares. The third way is through real estate. Farmland, industrial land, or commercial property made these people some of the richest.

Who didn't make the list? Not one of the 400 acquired wealth by the passing down of a large lump or trainload of a thing. Not one family made the list by owning a large amount of a commodity and letting it compound over several generations. Why? Because commodities don't appreciate relative to inflation. Think about this. Next time a talking head tries to sell you gold, call that 800 number and tell them not one of the richest people in America has ever gotten rich from gold!

Second, Buffett discussed his thoughts on gold during a CNBC interview in October 2013. He said if you took all the gold in the world, it would create a cube 67 feet high by 67 feet wide by 67 feet long.

The total value of that gold at the time of the interview was about $7 trillion. He said for the same amount of money, he could own all of the farmland in the United States (about half the country) and seven Exxon Mobils, and still have $1 trillion of "walking around money" left over. He said, "Call me crazy, but I'll take the farmland and the seven Exxons." So would I. The annual income from those assets is billions of dollars. The annual income from gold is below $0, because of storage and insurance costs.

Why I Prefer Stocks to Real Estate

I own some real estate. Some is in my residence, and some in a vacation home and one piece of land. Other than that, I own all my other real estate through REITs—real estate investment trusts, which function similarly to mutual funds—because it's the most convenient option. You don't have to do anything but invest with the right experts, who have a lot of capital and knowledge. No property taxes, no zoning problems, and no renter problems. You *will* miss out on all those interesting homeowner's association meetings. I think you can live without them.

Stocks don't have roofs, toilets, termites, or mold problems.

Unlike real estate, stocks have a level playing field. The transaction costs are almost nothing nowadays and they are fair. No hidden costs. When I buy a share of stock, it is exactly the same as the share the billionaire owns.

There is nothing wrong with owning your own commercial property or rentals. They just aren't for me. First of all, I am not at all handy. I can't fix much of anything and don't really want to. I love to hear people who own rentals regaling how they spent a whole weekend fixing stuff and then conclude that it was free because they did it themselves. If they count their time as zero value, I guess they are right. Don't fall into that trap. Keep track of your time and value it at whatever you normally make. You may do better working more and investing it.

Second, I am not good with dealing with tenants who are late in paying or have damaged my property. I just don't have the temperament for it. If you love to tinker and fix things, and you don't get upset with constantly finding new tenants and doing repairs, you can make money. I believe you would make a lot more in REITs, either in the form of stocks or private offerings. Both have advantages, and you need to make the decision that's right for your situation.

Many people who own rentals have them for the tax advantages that are available, which can be valuable. Me? I don't want to keep track of that stuff and I don't want to get audited. The whole residential rental thing is way too much drama for my tastes. That is the way I think, but I am a financial planner, so naturally I am more comfortable in what I know. Stocks don't have roofs, toilets, termites, or mold problems. I like that.

Some people just enjoy owning rentals like I enjoy owning companies. They like to be hands on. In that case, as long as you enjoy it and the math works, you're all set.

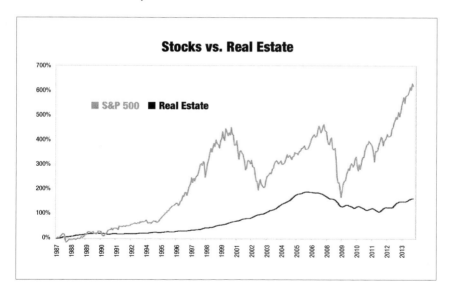

Chapter 3 Takeaways:

1. Staying even with inflation won't make you wealthy. You will never create serious wealth investing in bonds or bank deposits.

2. There is no connection between the mechanism that prices your stock (random votes of everyone with a computer or phone) and the actual value of one share of a company.

3. If you are under 85 years old, you experienced the worst stock-market event in your life in 2008. You lived.

4. A once-in-a-lifetime opportunity to pick up stocks at prices way below their actual value was in 2009. There will be several more exceptional buying opportunities coming up before you are done.

5. With any luck, you could be the "Unluckiest Investor in the World."

Mindful Money Questions:

1. What are three common, accurate, and easy ways to keep track of inflation?

2. Why do stocks go up in value over long periods?

3. How are commodities different from equity assets?

CHAPTER 4

Faith and Patience Are the Two Keys to Investor Success

"The Market is the great allocator, from the impatient to the patient."

—Warren Buffett

"In certain years you'll earn your 30%, but there will be other years when you you'll only make 2%, or perhaps you will lose 20%. That's part of the scheme of things and you have to accept it…if you expect 30%…you're more likely to get frustrated…and your impatience may cause you to abandon your stocks at precisely the wrong moment."

—Peter Lynch, *One Up on Wall Street*

Let me start by saying that 25 seconds is not a long time. Neither is 25 days, weeks, or months. In terms of investing, 25 years or more is a long time. Over the course of my career, I have seen this industry change from long-term thinking to instant gratification. When you click on a chart for a stock, the default is *one day.* How is it helpful to know what a stock sold for while you were in the bathroom? Unfortunately, there are people who think it matters a lot. My advice? Go ahead, leave your smartphone on your desk, and take the bathroom break. You won't have missed anything.

If you are a baby boomer like me, you know that 25 years goes by very quickly—and the next 25 will be quicker. If you are 55 now, you will be 80. If you think you won't care about money at 80 or 90, you had better think again. When our oldest client—103 years old!—calls our firm, we tell her the same thing we tell everyone: Be patient. The money will go to her heirs and be invested for decades more. Even when you are so old you won't risk buying green bananas, you need to be patient.

Peter Lynch said to check your stocks like you check the oil in the car—but I'd suggest even that is too often if you do a lot of driving like we do out West. I would tell you to check your stocks as often as you check your transmission fluid. If you can't remember the last time you did that, you get the idea.

The First Key: *Faith*

This is not in the sense of religious faith, or faith in something that cannot be demonstrated. It is faith in an economic fact. That is, in general, you must have faith that things are going to become more expensive and more valuable over time. This seems intuitive, but it is not. Very few people will follow this established law, which is as sure as many physical laws we rely on every day. If I sit down in a chair, I trust it will hold my weight. I put my *faith* in the chair and the laws of physics.

Unfortunately, people have less faith when it comes to money. They have no problem sitting in the chair or thinking their favorite college football team could beat the Green Bay Packers, but when it comes to faith that Starbucks will sell more coffee, or Costco is going to sell more goods in the future, it is not something they are able, psychologically, to act on. And I don't believe it has anything to do with logic. It is just plain old garden-variety fear. "But our generation is different!" they say. Just look at the younger generation! Look at the economy! Our national debt! You can fill in the blank with latest crisis du jour.

What they forget is that they are just channeling the thoughts of every generation. My parents hated Led Zeppelin every bit as much as I dislike rap music. It is a mental trick, nothing more, to believe that it is "all over." The future fiscal failure says, "I understand what you are saying about Costco/Starbucks/Company X, but what *you* don't see is that this time it's different" because of some political, economic, religious, or superstitious reason. I'll sit and not-so-patiently listen to their particular theory, but I'm going to put my faith in reality, and the knowledge that life will go on.

I wrote a book in 1998 titled *Y2K, We're OK, Why the Millennium Bug Won't Bite*. I wrote it because I was dismayed by the overreactions of investors to what I thought was an obviously silly event. On New

Year's Day 2000, there was 0.00% chance of a disaster. That could have been easily known. What kept it from being easily known? Magical thinking: superstition of the millennial change. Fear and greed, stoked by the media who makes their living on those things. Fear and greed by charlatans peddling survival supplies and voodoo-based investment theories. Fear by people buying into the panic. It was mass hysteria at its finest.

And, as always, "This time it's different" lost again.

During that time, I learned a lot. I learned which clients were rational enough to be successful, and who were the Elevator Guys. I decided that we wouldn't work with the latter. Two thoughts always came to mind in that period: 1) You can lead a horse to water, but you can't make him drink. I was worn out by leading those horses. 2) You can't teach a pig to sing; you'll get frustrated and it will irritate the pig. I was tired of giving singing lessons. We decided as a firm that we were not going to hydrate stubborn horses or create pig choirs anymore. If someone insisted on selling at the bottom, we couldn't work with them.

We went through our clients and removed the ones who were eating up all of our time, energy, and emotional stamina. Our client roster went from more than 300 households to 140 households, practically overnight. That was a good start—but it was a very scary thing. I had been advised for years that overly fearful clients would kill my business. I had heard that business would improve if I learned to use boundaries and not succumb to hand wringers. Sure enough, business has been better and we are having a lot more fun working with rational folks.

Whether you are a client or not, I want you to be on the alert to prevent bad investment behavior—not just for one event like Y2K, but for any event that makes you think "this time it's different." Quit allowing such occurrences to sabotage your wealth over and over. Take the steps to overcome the biggest enemy of investing success and wealth accumulation: your own brain.

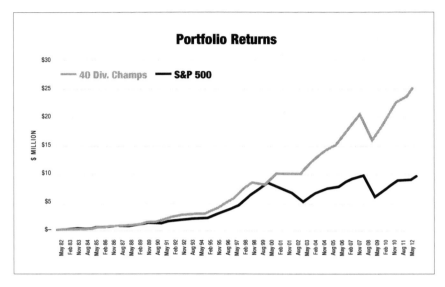

You can be confident that the way out of this mental dilemma is in this book. Some of the best minds in investment psychology and the neuroscience of changing your brain have been consulted in this project.

Is there ever a compelling reason we shouldn't do wise things with our money because of fear of disaster in the future? The fact is *there will be a disaster in the future*. And it won't stop the world from moving on and equity assets going up in value over time.

But what about hyperinflation, stagflation, deflation, unrest in the Middle East, confiscation of assets by the government, floods and droughts, hordes of deadbeats collecting government handouts, unemployment, labor shortages, famine, nuclear accidents, terrorism, devaluation of the dollar, takeover of the government by Muslim terrorists, FEMA putting us in concentration camps, aliens attacking, anarchy, rap music, religious fundamentalism, runaway national debt, quantitative easing, moral decay, rampant drug use, cloning, runaway viruses, melting of the polar ice caps, genetically modified food, famine, pestilence, rioting, gay marriage, breakdown of the family structure, invasive species, rodent infestation, slippery sidewalks, no mail delivery on Saturday, smaller ice cream cartons, smaller dog food bags, teenage acne, athlete's foot, and acid reflux? Phewwww! Turn off the news!

Oh, by the way, do you think Starbucks will sell more coffee,

Costco will sell more goods, and computers will be faster and cheaper in 20 years? That is what is called refocusing. When your brain gets the equivalent of uncontrolled high-velocity diarrhea as in the above paragraph, you need to refocus. Attention on right thoughts is a key to the *Mindful Money* process.

Is the Market Rigged?

A lot of people will ask me how to have faith when the market is rigged or that a small group of people are pulling strings behind the scenes. *The Da Vinci Code* may have popularized the concept, but the truth is that the conspiracy theories have been around for centuries and involve shadowy secret societies like the "Illuminati" or the "Trilateral Commission." In the financial world, two of the biggest targets of conspiracy theories are the Federal Reserve and high-frequency trading. Neither of these will determine the price of Starbucks or Costco in 20 years. The only thing that will matter is: Has Starbucks sold more coffee, increased earnings, and paid more dividends than it did 20 years ago? Same question for Costco. That's it. No conspiracies, just more reasons to keep from investing.

You must be mindful of these red herrings when they come by and keep you from investing. When you watch "60 Minutes" and *Flash Boys* author Michael Lewis is harping about "high-speed trading," it can make you wonder. But, again: How does that affect what the earnings of companies are in the future? Not at all.

The short answer is no, the market is not rigged. We have the most efficient market in the history of the planet. If Buffett buys a share of Coca-Cola and I buy a share at precisely the same moment, we get the same deal. There is no advantage for the rich guy, even one who owns a lot of KO like Buffett does.

Now, what about high-speed trading, options, futures, etc.? Are they rigged? My answer is not really. Let's look at an example and you tell me if it's rigged or not.

You are selling your house for $875,000 and receive two offers. The first is for full price, contingent on the buyer closing on his current house and his bank approving a loan. The second offer is for $865,000 in the form of a cashier's check; you can close today. Which one is more attractive? If you picked offer number one, that would be very strange. Almost all of us would take the sure deal with cash in hand.

Question: Was your house deal rigged in favor of the cash-rich buyer? His ability to pay in full with no contingencies gave him an advantage. Well, guess what: Anyone in America or wherever who has lots of capital has an advantage! For instance, they have enough money to get the very best price on stocks. Same goes for bonds. The wealthy get lots of discounts in various forms. They can buy the technology that we can't even think about. As a result, they gain a slight advantage. Does that change the price of Wal-Mart stock 10 years from now? No.

The factors that people point to as market-rigging will have almost zero effect on the price of your portfolio when you retire or need it for one of life's big events.

The Second Key: *Patience*

An old college friend used to say with regularity: "Craig, you are the world's most impatient man." He had me nailed. Thirty-plus years later, I am not particularly patient, but I am patient enough to survive and I am slowly but surely improving my ability. Until I appreciated the power of patience, I never really understood much of anything. Most things in life will turn out all right if we simply wait.

The placebo effect in medicine is largely based on patience. The majority of ailments will go away with time, as will many of your problems.

While researching this book, I met with Dr. Tony Lucas from University of Nevada, Las Vegas, head of the school's gaming department. He tells me that the number-one reason people lose so much money is that they don't have enough patience to capture the already lousy odds they have at the slot machine or card game. They hate to fold a hand or stand pat in blackjack. Impatience is the bread and butter of the gaming industry. You don't get those nice soaps and shampoos from gamblers who exercise patience. When you own stocks, you are the casino. Gravity is on your side. Good companies get more valuable over time. Casinos have all the patience because they know the odds going in. Sometimes they have a streak of bad luck when they actually lose. Do they worry? No, the odds will always win, as will the growth of good companies and well-located real estate.

If one of those problems is a low account balance on your last investment statement, patience is just what the doctor ordered. Not long before this book went to press, we passed the five-year anniversary of the Dow being under 7,000 points—and today, it is in the neighborhood of 20,000. What would a value investor have done five years ago, with stocks priced at such historically low P/E ratios and high dividends? He would have purchased more. He would have kept purchasing on the way down, not because of some magical number or chart, but stocks would have been purchased when they were deemed to be of fair value for the long run.

Good investments are owned by smart investors because they are quality assets. They have a reliable history and a good probability of continuing to do so after careful analysis. This is true for individual stocks, real estate, or baskets of stocks or real estate owned by buying a mutual fund, index fund, or other managed pool of assets.

If those investments go up in the short term, that doesn't mean you were right. If they go down, it doesn't mean you were wrong. In fact, it won't matter. They will go up if you have the patience. It is the gnawing feeling that things will continue to go down, or the false euphoria of a quick move up, that results in people failing to accumulate and maintain wealth. They will either sell too quickly, or insist that they put more money in the assets that are going up. That will become their Achilles' heel.

The notion that stocks are going up or going down is another faulty thought. They have done what they have done. What they have done up until one second ago has no predictive power of where they are headed next. But if you watch the financial channels on TV, at least once a day you'll hear someone say that either stocks are "going up" or "going down."

It is the same with real estate or anything else. Your property is never going up or down. It is the value it is, period. It may have gone up or gone down, but you have no idea where it is going. You may have the nagging thought that if you sell something it will shoot up in price. You may also feel if you buy something it will go down. I know people who think that because they bought or sold something it jinxed the investment and changed the course of that investment. We all know that it's silly, but "this is just my luck" is a logical fallacy (error of extrapolation) and a thinking error (emotional reasoning). These are deadly thoughts for our portfolios.

As we have said, almost all equity derives from companies or real estate. Equity cannot be created by government. Government can only act as a carburetor on equity, by creating the right balance of capital to labor. At its best, government allows labor and capitalists to participate in the ownership of equity through free and efficient real estate and stock markets.

The notion that stocks are going up or going down is another faulty thought. They have done what they have done. What they have done up until one second ago has no predictive power of where they are headed next.

What is not an equity asset: bonds and bank deposits. Equity requires ownership. Companies and mortgages cannot loan out capital at a rate than less they will make on that capital. Consider that a law. As mentioned earlier, commodities are not capital assets and do not appreciate consistently relative to inflation.

Even with lousy government, money can still be made in equities and real estate. But with bad government comes over-control of capitalists or over-control of labor. You only have to look at China, India, and Russia as examples of poor government policy. Within each of these countries, fortunes can still be made. But only people with capital will participate; the fewer people that participate, the worse the long-term prospects are for the economy.

It has only been since China embraced free markets that the standard of living for their people has skyrocketed. Standard of living up, more goods and services purchased. If they clamp down on free markets, growth will be restrained by fewer people participating. If they let free markets run wild, growth will be restrained by fewer people participating. Striking a good balance creates the environment for growth. That is why the U.S. leads the world. The balance is never perfect nor always good, but we realize that both capital and labor must be protected.

No matter which way the weight of capital versus labor swings, someone is not happy. This brings up another major mental error committed by the average investor: getting sidetracked from the basic laws of wealth by ruminating on things you have no way of changing. We need to know what we can change and what we cannot change, and the latter is a very long list. What we can change is how *we think*.

Consider my dog. He is looking out the window and shaking like a leaf because he wants to go chase the raccoon that is outside. I will never let him chase that rabies-infested thing, but he sits and suffers for no reason. But he's a dog. You are not. You know better than to chase dumb ideas. You can also train yourself by employing *Mindful Money* to not shake like a leaf the next time your barber tells you he knows about a stock that is a "sure thing." Change the subject to sports or hairspray. Don't be tempted by that rabies-infested stock.

I tell clients, when they are wringing their hands over politics, they have only three things they can do: 1) They can roll up their sleeves or open the checkbook to support the cause; 2) they can vote; or 3) they can pray. Beyond that, they are wasting their time and emotional energy and being distracted from what is permanent by what is the headline of the day.

We no longer have the luxury of hearing all of the news in the world in less than 30 minutes from old-school newsmen like Walter Cronkite or Chet Huntley and David Brinkley. We no longer have the luxury of hearing the news without commentary that we really don't need. We do have the option of wisely choosing the news we absorb and turning off the news we shouldn't. Financial media does not exist to help you get wealthy; it exists to draw viewers with entertainment and to sell advertising.

Financial media on TV is not a public service. It is a business, a show, competing against all other entertainment. If they told you to buy quality assets and to ignore short-term events, they would be out of business. Magazines aren't much better. They have to put content in every week. The very nature of the business is to convince you that you have to constantly be reacting and changing direction. I'm not saying that they don't believe what they say. I am just saying it doesn't work.

> ***We no longer have the luxury of hearing***
> ***all of the news in the world in less than 30 minutes from old-school***
> ***newsmen like Cronkite or Huntley and Brinkley.***

As for the Internet, it is the most useful tool to come along for the investor. It can also be the most damaging, because it requires you to choose the right information over the wrong, and the truth-tellers over the charlatans. Both the Internet and TV abound with what I would call pure crooks: people who know they are cheating you when they start out, as opposed to sincere people who are wrong. Morally, they are worlds apart. To your bottom line, however, there is no difference.

You may think that I have rose-colored glasses on, and think everything will be OK, and that nothing catastrophic will ever happen. Not true, false, false. I am really not all that optimistic. (Ask my wife and business associates.) In fact I am quite negative, thank you. But I have learned to know what I can control and what is worth my worry and what is not.

I have also learned that in any era, even true catastrophes are opportunities in a long-term plan. I tell myself, "This too shall pass," even if it may be long and painful. And if this time, it *really is* different, we will all be dead or in a world that we know nothing of, and cannot plan for anyway. Gravity may also go away and I may float away from my computer. I am just not going to plan for it.

Chapter 4 Takeaways:

1. "Yeah, but this time it really IS different." No, it's not.

2. Don't watch financial media, even for entertainment or torture or whatever other reason. They are not there to give you good long-term advice. If they were, they would be out of business.

3. Stocks and real estate are never "going up" or "going down." They are where they are at this moment. We have no idea where they are going.

4. Remember the illusion of understanding and the illusion of validity.

5. What we cannot change is a very long list. What we can change is *how we think*.

Mindful Money Questions:

1. What is a Huntley or a Brinkley?

2. Do we have the ability to know future events?

3. Are gold, silver, or pork bellies equity assets?

4. Can you ever tell if stocks are going up or down?

CHAPTER 5

Can We Know We Are Doing the Right Thing?

"Don't let Wall Street scam you, like I did."
—Bernie Madoff, currently serving a 150-year term
at Butner Federal Correctional Institution

Can we trust financial analysts? The answer is a resounding "no"!
Analysts are worse at predicting stock prices than guessing. Why is
this? First of all, the media and analysts are no different from you
and me. They panic or get overconfident, and always at the wrong
time. Looking at Yahoo! Finance, you will see 30 or 40 analysts
covering most well-known stocks. The price predictions they make
are always—or almost always—12 months from now. It's a guessing
game that can make or break an analyst. We will never know how
many really good analysts have gotten fired over bad luck, but it is a
lot. An old Wall Street joke says that the most common word attached
to analyst estimates is "surprise."

Let's use an example. In May 2015, oil was trying to recover from
a huge crash in price that started in October of the previous year. A
barrel of oil was around $100 in September, hit a low of around $40
around the first of the year, and rose to $60 by May. So the drop was
a once-in-a-decade opportunity to buy oil stocks in my opinion.
A company I own and follow, Nabors Industries (NBR), is a large
drilling and oil services company. The initial drop in oil was a 60%
drop! The recovery from 40 to 60 is a 50% gain. We bought Nabors in
October and continued to buy to the bottom. We have done very well
at this point.

So, here's the news headline:

UBS Says to Buy the Big 3 Land Drillers Now
May 7, 2015 9:05 am EDT

Translation: The analysts want you to buy Nabors Industries *now*.

And now, the article:

> The UBS price target is $19, and the consensus price objective is
> $16.71. Shares closed most recently at $16.33.

Nabors hit a low of $9.91 in early 2015. Now they wanted you to buy
it, after it was up more than 65%! They have a hopeful "price target" of
$19. As usual, this rearview-mirror investing is useless for the investor.
Investor, if you want to make money, don't wait for the analysts to tell
you. They only recommend a stock after they see in the rearview mirror
that it has recovered.

How did this recommendation turn out for investors? Shares of
Nabors are now (in December of 2016) at $16.31. The one year "target"
was not reached. My point here is that by the time analysts are gushing
over a stock, it usually is past the point of its maximum potential.
Financial media has almost no predictive power!

If you want to make money, you will buy at the point of optimum
pessimism. You want to own a company when most others are terrified,
not after it has recovered 65%! I wish I could tell you this type of analyst
advice is an outlier. It is not—it is what they do. They want to play it
safe. Now when someone walks in a UBS office all they will see is that
NBR is on the recommended list. You go look it up and see it is up 70%
and think, "Wow, that was a good call!" Unless you research it, you will
never know they just added it to the list.

The individual investor has an advantage here. Analysts are always
under pressure to do something no one can do: predict the future.
Furthermore, their jobs are on the line and they are paid well. At our
firm, we have no such pressure—nor do you as an individual investor.
We tell clients up front that we are going to buy the best companies

we can find and let them appreciate. Buffett has said, "We (Berkshire Hathaway) do not have, will not have, and never had any idea of where the market interest rates or the business cycle will be 12 months from now." Serious investors don't care and shouldn't care. You want to buy the stock as if you were buying the whole company. If you want to do the right thing, you should buy great businesses and let them operate.

I recently read another article on analysts' predictions on oil prices. The article said 50% thought prices were going up and 50% thought they were going down. Now let's think about this! It is funny because the answer is that oil prices will go up. And 100% of the analysts should say that oil will go up in the long run, and over the long run is what we need to care about. Thousands of people read that article, and I bet very few would see the humor in the prediction unless it was pointed out. Be able to read these things and smile.

The Internet: An Amazing Tool

There is no website that I know of that will give you stock picks that will get you a great portfolio. In my opinion, sites like the Motley Fool or Seeking Alpha are not helpful. They are trying to sell stuff to you on every click. The demand to come up with ideas every day for years is too much. A good portfolio should only contain 20 to 50 stocks. So how can a website that pitches that many stocks each week be of help? Motley Fool or Seeking Alpha can be a good source of *ideas*—a starting point, not an ending point. Always have a lot of ideas. My rule of thumb is that you can follow about 200 stocks. When you get to that number, kick one out before you add more.

What about newsletters? Newsletters, like all financial media, are there not to make you money but to make the publisher money. Their track records are not good. There is really no way to get an accurate track record, because each issue has new ideas and you have a moving target. There are some that are better than others, although you still need to ask: Why pay for a newsletter when you can now see the top holdings of the best long-term value investors on many websites?

Good decisions are usually made by individuals, not groups. If you have served on a board, you have surely experienced this.

Congress cannot decide on much—too many opinions. Do the boards that have operated for Steve Jobs, Warren Buffett, Jeff Bezos, or Meg Whitman, control the ultimate decisions of these brilliant leaders? A good decision-maker will distinguish easily between good advice and rubbish. These people are examples of people who will listen to good advice, but ultimately make the right decision in most cases.

Make your own decisions. Hold your own counsel. Be rational. Always ask, "Is this true?" You know you can Google it, but that is a dangerous world. Always remember the Elevator Guy. Google may just add to the problem, if you're looking for articles where the elevators *have* fallen. Search "Is the market rigged?" or "Is the United States finished?" or "Should I buy gold?" and you will find what you are looking for.

There will be some convincing-looking websites and logical-sounding articles that say you should not vaccinate your kids, the elevator is due to fall, the market is rigged, the U.S. is done, or the government covers up UFOs. If you shop for the answer you want, you will get it. That is the nature of the Internet. And when you find that article that "proves" Hillary Clinton or Dick Cheney or anyone else is the Antichrist, please think about it carefully before you send it out to your whole email list.

Make your own decisions.
Hold your own counsel. Be rational.
Always ask, "Is this true?"

Another good place to start is Wikipedia, which supplies fairly reliable information. The fact that it is edited by about 1,400 editors, and that anyone can apply to be an editor, is very helpful in cleaning up bad information. Compilers of articles such as Real Clear Markets and Real Clear Politics let you choose from a wide variety of sources. The most important choice you can make, however, is who to hire as your financial advisor if you need one.

What Is a Theory? And How Does Long-term Value Investing Rate?

Investment techniques are proven (or disproven) like any other idea. The process starts with a *hypothesis*. This initial thought or idea is not yet a *theory*. It is studied and tested over a long period. If it works over and over, the theory becomes widely accepted—but it is not yet a law. You never hear anyone talk about the "law of evolution" because by its nature, proving evolution is impossible. For science to declare something a law, it must be observable and repeatable now and forever. You will hear the "law of gravity" or the "law of thermodynamics" because they are testable. Many things that you accept as fact every day are really considered theories.

Some examples:

Germ Theory: During the Civil War, more people died of infection than from being shot, stabbed, or blown up by cannons. At that time, the idea of infection being spread by germs was not known. Doctors didn't wash their hands before trying to repair wounds. Then the idea came about. It was studied over decades, and became germ theory. Even though it is now accepted pretty much by everyone, there are still people who deny the cause-and-effect relationship between germs and disease; most of them are into some sort of alternative medicine. Many who don't accept germ theory believe the disease causes the microorganisms, not the other way around. One well-known advocate of this form of denialism is comedian and political commentator Bill Maher, who has claimed that Pasteur recanted germ theory on his deathbed. This is the root of the antivaccine movement, which is not based on fact, but fear.

Calorie Theory: As I mentioned in the Introduction, it was not until the 1920s that the first book on dieting by counting calories was published. If, 100 years ago, your cousin was on his third sausage burger and you told him to not eat so many calories, he would have looked at you like you were from Jupiter. So, the truth doesn't change, it just gets discovered. As scientists studied it for decades, the idea became a theory, and then it became a strong theory or even would be called a fact. Even so, there are still plenty of "calorie deniers" who are not convinced that calories are a component of weight loss or gain. For me, calorie reduction is the only way I have ever been able to lose weight. For me, it is proven!

Theory of Relativity: How would you even begin to guess this? Then Albert Einstein popped in and told us that if you got into a spaceship and traveled at the speed of light for a billion years, you would not get any older. Really? Who's gonna believe that? Well, now it has been observed, calculated, and determined that the crazy dude with the bad hair was probably right. No one guesses the truth in advance; it is just too odd. The theory can be observed, it can be shown mathematically, but I don't think science can tell us why it works.

The Big Bang Theory: Before World War II, the universe was believed by most scientists and the public as having existed forever. It was known as the Steady State Theory. By mid-century, there was a competing concept that the universe started with a big explosion all at once: i.e., the Big Bang Theory, which opened up people's thinking about the size and age of the universe. After a few decades of observation and reporting we knew the universe was huge, possibly infinite. Today, a new batch of scientists has proposed that the number of *universes themselves* could be infinite: a concept known as the *multiverse*. Infinity is a convenient tool when making up theories!

My point here is that science changes constantly. Each new "fact" can later be discovered to be nonsense. The consensus today, after 60 years of observations, is that the universe is expanding from a single point. Theorists say they can calculate its age to be around 13.8 billion years. Even so, there are people who believe in the Steady State Theory or alternate theories.

Never relax thinking that the consensus must be right. As Matt Ridley, author of numerous books on scientific topics, observes:

"Besides, science does not respect consensus. There was once widespread agreement about phlogiston (a nonexistent element said to be a crucial part of combustion), eugenics, the impossibility of continental drift, the idea that genes were made of protein (not DNA) and stomach ulcers were caused by stress, and so forth—all of which proved false. The famous physicist Richard Feynman once said, 'Science is the belief in the ignorance of experts.' "

The Danger of Consensus in the Investment World

Consensus is not very good predictor of accuracy. In fact, consensus can be a dangerous thing. While we think it is a noble goal, and it can be, not all opinions are equally weighted. The striving for consensus can lead to devastating results—such as when doing the right thing is ignored at the cost of everyone being in agreement. When taken to the extreme, it stifles dissent and creativity. Some people are convinced that government by referendum would be paradise. In fact, I believe it would be hell. Some famous politicians, including Ross Perot, have argued for the use of national referendums. Their thinking is that if everyone could just vote and let the majority rule, we'd be all set. I will let you use your imagination on this particular form of chaos: a nation in which the masses could instantly vote on how to proceed with life-and-death issues with a click of a mouse.

Now stop imagining it, and realize that's what happens every day in the stock market. The entire population of Internet users can change the direction of a stock. At any given point, we are in the midst of not one, but several media-induced crises. The Ebola virus, the new oil crisis (a world in which we have *too much* oil), and the daily reports on ISIS and their ability to take over the world. I would bet you that in two years, or even two months, these events will be given very little thought. But these things move the market. As Chevron stock fell from $134 a share to $105 a share, analysts cautioned to lighten up on Chevron and other oil stocks. Where were they when they could have helped us at $134? At a 30% discount, the consensus suddenly became a wait-and-see approach to Chevron.

The striving for consensus can lead to devastating results—
such as when doing the right thing is ignored
at the cost of everyone being in agreement.

There is always someone who can argue that nothing can be proven, which is why we are hesitant in science or medicine or financial analysis to say anything is 100% fact. Taken to its extreme: Since I have never been to Paris, how do I know it exists? The fact is, I don't. I believe it exists from the overwhelming evidence that I have. I have many friends who have been there, I have seen pictures, and I can conclude Paris is real. I can't *know* Paris is real, but the "Paris Theory" is as proven as it can get. For someone who has been isolated in the jungle their entire life, with no contact with the outside world, the idea of Paris being real would be a much longer journey than for someone with the facts.

The point is that things start out as thoughts or ideas and grow into theories. The theories become stronger or weaker. Strong theories are treated as fact, even though not proven. Right or wrong, the Theory of Relativity is now a strong theory. It has an overwhelming evidence (not just consensus) of science and it has the time of observation to disprove it—which hasn't been done and is probably not forthcoming. Ideas become theories; theories are tested and observed, sometimes over many decades. Then at some point they become either accepted or discarded.

Value Investing as a Theory

Open the Internet or a financial journal, and you may see articles that declare "Value Investing: a time-tested, proven strategy." And it is a proven strategy. But like other theories, it is just a theory. In fact, 100 years ago, most experts considered bonds as the best long-term investment; it is now widely regarded as fact that the owning of stocks over the long term is superior to holding bonds. It is hard to see in hindsight how things that are so obvious in our age were misunderstood in the past. And many of the things we believe today will be proven false long after we are dead.

The arithmetic is quite simple. Many corporations borrow money to expand and grow. Borrowing is called leverage. If you can borrow money at 5% and grow your business profits at 10%, then the borrowing is a good business decision. You can lever up your growth with other people's money. When a company issues bonds, they are *borrowing* money. When you purchase a bond you are *lending* money to that corporation. Let's say Boeing offers to pay you 4% interest for 10 years. That would be considered a high-quality corporate bond. Boeing has good credit and an overwhelming chance of paying you that 4% and then returning your $1,000 at the end of 10 years. $1,000 is usually the minimum bond purchase. These types of bonds are a reliable source of income and carry a guarantee of the return of your money backed by the creditworthiness of Boeing.

Now, let's look at the simple math. Boeing is willing to pay you 4% on your money. We can rest assured that Boeing is confident that they can grow their business at a rate higher than 4%. They cannot borrow money at 4% and grow at 2%, for instance. (At least not forever.) Eventually, companies that borrow at higher rates than they earn go broke, or default on the bond payments. If they are in risk of default and have a lower credit rating, they have to pay more to borrow. Let's say they have to pay 8%, due to their poor credit. This is what is known as a junk bond. They pay more, but carry a higher risk of default. At any rate, the point here is that companies cannot *borrow* money at rates higher than they can *grow*.

You have the choice of owning shares of a company (owning the stock) or loaning the money by buying one of their bonds. With our markets, you have that choice every day. A lot of people don't want to be owners. They want to be loaners. Even though the odds would obviously and mathematically be in their favor, they don't want to deal with the uncertainty of an owner. This uncertainty is nothing more than fluctuation. If you cannot tolerate that your investments will fluctuate with time, you will not be able to proceed with the creation of wealth. If you think you can grow your money at double-digit rates without fluctuation, you have believed a theory that says you can somehow avoid the fluctuations. In this case, I also believe that you will fail.

This brings us back to our original thesis that there is just no proof that there's some secret that billionaires have that allows them to have these risk-free, high-return investments. The wealthy may get cheaper fees and access to more complex investments. But complexity rarely helps. If you find someone touting 12–20% returns with no risk, you are surely dealing with a con man. Even worse, some far-out strategy may work for the short run before you finally lose your money. Now you have wasted your most precious commodity: time. The truth doesn't change, it just gets discovered over time. The process is not as fast as you may think.

We will show that just by participating in market returns you can build wealth. We have also shown that relatively few people choose that path. You have the chance to break that cycle of insanity now.

There are usually a few people that hang on to discredited theories. Think of people who claim the Earth is flat, or who still cling to conspiracy theories: for example, that George Bush was responsible for the World Trade Center attacks, or that there were multiple shooters in the Kennedy assassination. There are psychological reasons people cling to beliefs. The truth is complicated and has a lot of layers. Some people are able to come to the facts sooner. They are not necessarily smarter in terms of I.Q. It is determined by other characteristics of thinking that they have been born with and have developed through life experiences.

The truth doesn't change, it just gets discovered over time.
The process is not as fast as you may think.

In the investment-advising field, we run into all kinds of brains. Some brains are wired for long-term thinking and critical thinking. These people might be described as having good instincts or as having common sense in the investment world. When we meet them, we say, "This guy is thinking the right thoughts." I would like to meet more of them, since they are few and far between. They are a rare commodity and they are the guy in your foursome that has all the money. Why shouldn't that be you?

One More Time: "Dread Is Not a Strategy"

The favorite and most dangerous four words of investing are "This time it's different." This time is *not* different. Equity beats debt from now until the end. And we don't know the end. Each generation thinks the same illogical thoughts. They think things are getting worse. They think the next generation is inferior. They think the problems of their day are insurmountable. And they are always wrong.

This time is not different. Buying quality equity assets at fair prices and having them appreciate over time works. It is proven. But it is still theory. It can never be a law—and thank the Lord for that. For if it were, everyone would have the wisdom to employ it and the opportunity we have as equity owners (i.e., people able to accept fluctuation in real growth assets) would not be as great. Value investing is a very strong theory, indeed—right up there with germ theory. I wonder if Bill Maher believes in equity growing more than debt.

Chapter 5 Takeaways:

1. Have you made investments based alone on an analyst estimate?
2. Don't search for the answer you want, but look for the answer that may be right.
3. Buy companies as if you were buying the business, because you really are.
4. Take advantage of all the information available, but ultimately it is your decision.
5. If you don't trust yourself, find someone you trust to help.
6. Don't believe something just because it has a consensus.

CHAPTER 6

Technical Analysis and Other Things that Don't Work

"I realized that technical analysis didn't work when I turned the chart upside down and didn't get a different answer."

—Warren Buffett

A lot of people are just so afraid to invest that they don't. But many others will invest in outlandish schemes and forgo doing any actual investing. The same person that tries to convince you the world is ending and you should buy gold will invest in a scam in a heartbeat—as long as the scammer entices him with phrases like "You know you can't trust Wall Street" and "Do you want to make money whether the market goes up or down?" I have met more of these people than I care to recall. They have invested many times in their lives, and it has always been on some ridiculous scam. By the time they get to us, they just assume that everything is crooked.

For the person who thinks everything is a rip-off, the story will end badly. I have talked to people who have been so focused on fees that they never invest, because they don't want to get ripped off with fees. Well, fees happen. We pay for everything. Nothing good is free. If someone doesn't want to invest, one excuse is as good as the next.

So how do we know when we are looking at a scam? It really is very easy. First put greed on your radar. One of my favorite TV shows is "American Greed"—it's an amazing look at the depths of depravity people will go to in order to make money.

The show is not called "American Greed" just because of the con artists. It is also named after the people who give the money to the con artists, because no one would do these things without greed. It all goes back to the same old thought: "There must be a faster, easier, more sophisticated way—a way the only the 'inside' guys know about." I'm here to tell you, there are no inside guys, at least not legal ones. Martha Stewart can tell you all about trading on inside information. It is rare and illegal, and has nothing to do with how many F-150s Ford will sell next year.

Bernie Madoff never sold registered securities. He never was audited by an outside authority or required to do reporting under SEC guidelines. People who gave him their money, and many of them were famous and successful, knew that going in—or they certainly could have. The investments were made out of greed, plain and simple. People invest because of what they *think*. We do things we know deep, deep down aren't right. We are human. We want to believe that we have found something that others have not. We are greatly motivated by fear and greed. When I was young and dumb, I invested in stocks I was lied to about. I invested my hard-earned money not on what I knew, but on what I wanted to believe. Anyone with a computer could have got all they needed to know to not invest with Madoff.

In general, I would advise against investing in securities that aren't registered and covered by SIPC insurance. Madoff would never reveal anything about how he invested the money. It was a black box. All he told people was that he had a secret formula and he couldn't reveal it. "Investors" put their money into a blind pool. It was not based on reason. We do know that Madoff was a trader to start, but the SEC still does not know when he changed from trying to make the money legitimately to running a Ponzi scheme. They only say it was sometime in the late '90s.

In general, I would advise against investing in securities that aren't registered and covered by SIPC insurance.

We have to give permission to get scammed. The cons need us to participate. After we know we are scammed, what is the first thing we say and think? Something like, "I knew that guy was crooked" or "I know that sounded too good to be true." To get duped, we have to believe in things that are wrong and *we* make the choice. We have to take responsibility for our decisions or this won't work. Investment scams will always exist as long as we stay willing customers.

Pamela Meyer, author of *Lie Spotting,* says, "A lie has no power whatsoever by its mere utterance, its power emerges when someone else agrees to believe it....lying is a cooperative act."

We live in the age of the victim, blaming our outcomes in life on whoever or whatever will ease the pain of taking responsibility for our thoughts and actions. We all do it. It is part of being human. When you agree to take your family's money and give it to a criminal or an incompetent person to invest, who are you going to blame? The criminal is in the business of lying; he probably won't take the blame. The incompetent person is eliminated by definition, so who does that leave?

Managed Futures and Trend Followers

You've all seen the commercials: "Make money whether the market goes up or down!" They want to sell you their system for making money on the options, just like the big guys on Wall Street! There are no "big guys." The problem is that this stuff doesn't work. Never has. Why do I say this?

There is no fund or pooled account that I am aware of or have been able to find that uses these strategies and makes a killing. Most of the returns in managed futures and options are dismal. If you find one that does work, let me know—I want in! (Please follow the rules from chapter 1 regarding track records.)

In an advertisement for a self-proclaimed "Super Trader" system, you see the headline claim: **How to Profit Again and Again...Taking Less Risk...in All Markets, Up or Down!** The text goes on to say:

Now you can start standing on the outside looking in. World Famous Super Trader reveals the secrets and advantages of options trading...just like the privileged insiders have. They are the traders who have seats on the CBOE Mercantile Exchange, where they take advantage of a secret- yet-legal rip-off that happens every day...they know where and when the next big moves will be!

Expect winning trades of 75%-85% of the time....holding positions for 30–90 days...and earning profits of at least 65-75% on each win (with a few "inside secret" mega profits thrown in, too!)

Notice the language in this advertisement. It is emotionally charged, using words like "insiders," "rip-off," and "secrets." Thank goodness—someone is going to reach out to you with the secret insider information! All of this is designed to make you think that the system is rigged for the big guys, the insiders, etc. The only thing Joe Doakes in Dubuque, Iowa, needs to do is fork over a few thousand and he will be rich in a year!

Until now these "experts" have been unwilling to talk outside their own circle of associates. They know where and when the next big moves will be! That's huge! Let's do this! This truly must be our lucky day! This stuff is not ridiculous until you think about it a minute, and that is what you need to do with scams and false ads. You need to step back and take a deep breath.

My first assumption in all cases is that I am self-deluded. That is my default. I would recommend you make it yours.

Let's go ahead, do the math, and we'll use all the worst-case-scenario figures: This system offers "winning trades" 75% of the time. He holds positions a maximum of 90 days. The ad says profits will be at *least* 65% on each "win." We'll ignore the few "inside secret" mega-profits "thrown in, too!"

75% times 65% equals a 48.75% return every 90 days. There are about four 90-day periods per year. Just to be conservative, we won't compound those during the year. So, a full year of trading would give us about a 195% gain—although that is really going low for what it tells us we could expect from a best-case scenario.

For context, consider that the wealthiest human has about $65 billion. The example below tells us that by using this system, we could be the richest human in the world in 24 years… by investing $1! (See figure 2.)

By starting with just $1 and getting the returns advertised, you would be as rich as Bill Gates—with more than $60 billion.

So maybe, just maybe, we can conclude that such claims are total nonsense. It is false advertising. It is just not true. I can't make this stuff up. Claims like these should be easily dismissed as ridiculous.

If someone could truly make 195% a year, do you think they would be hawking books and newsletters on TV?

Year	Deposits	Interest	Total Deposits	Total Interest	Balance
1	$0.00	$1.95	$1.00	$1.95	$2.95
2	$0.00	$5.75	$1.00	$7.70	$8.70
3	$0.00	$16.97	$1.00	$24.67	$25.67
4	$0.00	$50.06	$1.00	$74.73	$75.73
5	$0.00	$147.68	$1.00	$222.41	$223.41
6	$0.00	$435.66	$1.00	$658.07	$659.07
7	$0.00	$1,285.19	$1.00	$1,943.26	$1,944.26
8	$0.00	$3,791.30	$1.00	$5,734.56	$5,735.56
9	$0.00	$11,184.35	$1.00	$16,918.91	$16,919.91
10	$0.00	$32,993.83	$1.00	$49,912.75	$49,913.75
11	$0.00	$97,331.80	$1.00	$147,244.55	$147,245.55
12	$0.00	$287,128.82	$1.00	$434,373.37	$434,374.37
13	$0.00	$847,030.02	$1.00	$1,281,403.39	$1,281,404.39
14	$0.00	$2,498,738.56	$1.00	$3,780,141.95	$3,780,142.95
15	$0.00	$7,371,278.76	$1.00	$11,151,420.71	$11,151,421.71
16	$0.00	$21,745,272.33	$1.00	$32,896,693.04	$32,896,694.04
17	$0.00	$64,148,553.38	$1.00	$97,045,246.42	$97,045,247.42
18	$0.00	$189,238,232.47	$1.00	$286,283,478.90	$286,283,479.90
19	$0.00	$558,252,785.80	$1.00	$844,536,264.70	$844,536,265.70
20	$0.00	$1,646,845,718.11	$1.00	$2,491,381,982.80	$2,491,381,983.80
21	$0.00	$4,858,194,868.41	$1.00	$7,349,576,851.21	$7,349,576,852.21
22	$0.00	$14,331,674,861.81	$1.00	$21,681,251,713.03	$21,681,251,714.03
23	**$0.00**	**$42,278,440,842.35**	**$1.00**	**$63,959,692,555.38**	**$63,959,692,556.38**

Figure 2   Courtesy of *The Calculator site http://www.thecalculatorsite.com*

The ad copy above is based on claims made by widely watched people on CNBC. Why would these guys be touted as experts? I really don't know. I suppose some people like them and find them entertaining and interesting. I think CNBC is in the business of making you think there are ways to make money that are secret. If making money is public information (and it is) why would you need financial media?

You may ask, "Can people just get on TV and make stuff up?" Absolutely! It happens all the time. You have seen ads for all kinds of products on TV that don't live up to the hype. Do you really believe investments are any more honest? No true professional money manager would be on TV doing ads to give you his "secrets." There are no secrets, just imaginations run amok.

Keep in mind, if what they had advertised actually worked, it wouldn't work for long—because a great many people would pile in on the action. Secret plans are worthless once they aren't secret any longer.

Another reason we can know it doesn't work is because, if it did, there would be enormous profits in using it to manage money and, in turn, to sell the money-management services for way more than the book. Hedge funds charge 2% on all assets under management and then an additional 20% on gains. That's a lot of money, and sure-fire annual returns of 195% would be the quickest way to make it.

If CNBC came on the air every hour and told you to buy quality companies and hang on to them, how would they stay in business? They couldn't. Thus, it has become a whole industry built out of the illusion that there is some information you can get from CNBC (or any other financial broadcasts) to keep the whole game going. To me, there is no difference between CNBC and the Psychic Friends Network.

I'll even play devil's advocate: "What if it does work and I miss out?" How could it be true that CNBC features people every day who make a living selling outlandish schemes with exaggerated claims? You hope they don't, and you wish they wouldn't, but in fact they do. The whole point of financial media is to get you to buy more financial media and make you hungry for useless information. That's where the money is. If we started a rival network to tell people to buy quality assets and hang on, we'd be out of business the first week. Brokerage firms, especially the do-it-yourself ones, and financial media stake their future on getting you to think you have to trade rapidly. It is self-serving for them to make you think this.

When the online brokerage firms started out, they had some good points, mostly in terms of costs. They were way cheaper than conventional brokers by a multiple of 10, 20, or more per trade. Then costs came down. Today, everything is about active trading. You're made to feel stupid if you aren't "smart enough" to constantly trade.

Brokers used to get in trouble for trading too much. Today, we get scrutinized for not trading.

Could it be true that CNBC features people every day who make a living selling outlandish schemes with exaggerated claims? You hope they don't, and you wish they wouldn't, but in fact they do.

Last but not least, there are no funds using whatever strategy that these people are trying to sell you. We have already seen that they can turn $1 into $60 billion. That means they could turn $10 into $600 billion and $1,000 into $6 trillion. If they just had $3,000 to start, they could wipe out the US national debt, which is about $18 trillion. The whole idea is just silly. But you have to grow and sharpen your B.S. detector for a while so that you will just let this stuff float on by.

Technical Analysis

Technical analysis purports to predict future price movements of stocks based on patterns that already happened. Chart gazers, over time, believe they have determined certain patterns that make stocks behave one way or another in the future. These patterns have gained huge followings, and as mentioned earlier in the chapter, have been adopted by bright people.

Technical analysis, in fact, is taught in some of the best business schools in the country. These include Harvard, the University Of Pennsylvania Wharton School of Business, UCLA, Notre Dame, New York University, and many, many others. Surely *they* must know it works. They must have checked it out. No, I am afraid they didn't. Academics aren't especially good at weeding out bad information. To their credit, many universities have dropped their technical analysis programs.

Many famous hedge fund managers have become billionaires because of a lucky guess. One manager struck it rich in 1987 on Black Monday, after taking a large bet that the market would drop. His return for that year was over 100%. Not surprisingly, the fund exploded and attracted a ton of money. He has never come close to the returns he achieved in 1987, but now you'll hear the word "legendary" in front of his name. Why do some fund managers make huge amounts of money using trend-following techniques and become rich and famous? Is it because of trading secrets or trend-following? I don't think so, because there are no investable funds that use trend-following that have demonstrated persistency of returns. To illustrate how managers get famous and draw billions in investment money in—and get filthy rich—let's make up a story.

Imagine a game is set up in which 10 million people flip coins all day long. The experiment is set up to determine if there are special people who can consistently flip heads. The study is looking for someone who is adept at flipping heads 20 times in a row. The game gets started and days pass. Finally, several people out of the millions of participants have flipped heads 20 times in a row. Some of them have done it more than once, making them really valuable in the study. After a few months, we have identified 30 people who have flipped heads 20 times in a row more than once.

The study ends, and we send home the other 9,999,970 with a plaque commemorating their participation. They will always know, however, they don't have what it takes to be a good flipper. The other 30 become media stars, paraded around on the "Today" show and "The Oprah Winfrey Show" as national heroes. We have identified people who have the skill to flip heads repeatedly and they should be proud. The president invites them to the White House, where they are treated as stars. The TV networks all bid for the rights to have these people demonstrate their skill on national TV. The president of NBC wins the bidding and declares that this will be the biggest night ever in reality TV.

The night finally comes, and the 30 chosen ones walk out on stage. Each one has a roll of brand-new pennies from the Denver Mint. They are brought, one roll for each super-flipper, in a small velvet pouch displaying the NBC logo. An official-looking guard from the mint walks over and carefully hands off the coins to the amazing flippers one at a time, as the crowd sits in anticipation. Then, with music by the Los Angeles Symphony, a countdown starts: Ten! Nine! Eight! Seven! Six! Five! Four! Three! Two! One! Let the flipping begin! The masters all begin to flip the coins. They continue to flip and flip through the entire two-hour special. No one seems to be flipping any significant number of heads in a row and the crowd loses interest. People all over the country change the channel so they don't miss "Duck Dynasty" or "Honey Boo Boo."

The network is distraught. This has been a fiasco. Why didn't it work? We know why: It's because the premise is flawed. Everyone forgets about the flippers and returns to life, right? Actually, that doesn't happen. People start to blame the network. The flippers were under too much pressure. These are our chosen ones, how dare you insinuate that they did it by luck! The pennies were different. The flippers could do it when they had the old pennies from the San Francisco Mint. They were cheated by having to use the new coins. Many of the flippers go on to become famous and write books about their skills. Some of them still consider themselves to have powers that others don't have. And they also have a following of true believers who will always think they are special.

That's the end of that story, but the story continues every day in the world of hedge funds or other funds who strike it rich with a certain formula. In our penny story, persistency of results couldn't be demonstrated. With funds, it's persistency of returns—and I will say once again, that is the problem. A lucky manager has his 20-heads-in-a-row moment. People flock to him and give him billions of dollars. Even though he is never able to repeat the return of that one year, he is proclaimed a hero, a folk legend. Usually these people will continue to trade and attract money, but the returns are dismal. Any fund that can make 100% in a year has to be taking undue risk.

Another common source of scams is back-testing, as discussed earlier. A lot of people claim illustrations of investment results that aren't investment results at all, but rather a computer readout of a hot formula that would have done what is illustrated. Of course, the problem here is that no one actually made any money off of the illustrated results. The computer keeps chugging away until it spits out a result that works. Then, the investment company will actually try to mirror that return with a mutual fund or other product that copies the successful strategy from the computer. In reality, the computer result was an anomaly—not something it's possible to build a strategy around.

You may also hear claims of a new algorithm that is the key to stock investing. It's all very impressive, with scores of PhDs cranking away at these formulas. Some of them even work for a short period of time. Consider the story below, quoted from the *Boston Globe*:

A longtime MIT business school professor and his son agreed to pay $4.8 million to settle federal securities charges that they misled investors in their Boston hedge fund company.

The Securities and Exchange Commission said Gabriel R. Bitran, a professor of operations management at the MIT Sloan School of

Management, and his son, Marco, raised millions of dollars for their
hedge funds by falsely telling investors they had a history of successfully
earning money, when the track record was based on hypothetical trades.

The SEC also accused the father-son team of persuading investors they
would use a sophisticated strategy the professor devised to invest in exchange-
traded funds and other securities, when they simply put the money in other
funds, including Bernard Madoff's mammoth pyramid scheme.

The agency also accused them of providing phony books and records
to government investigators looking into the firm.

The above story is all true. The men actually put the money with
Bernie Madoff after they realized they had no chance with their formula!
The funny part of it is that two operators of a Ponzi scheme got suckered
into a Ponzi scheme while trying to bail out their own Ponzi scheme.
Now, the not-so-funny part: Surely regulators would have stopped them
from doing business from then on, right? Wrong! They rebranded under
another name and have gone back into basically the same business
pitching more formulas.

The idea of people running Ponzi schemes investing themselves
in other Ponzi schemes may be more common than we know. It is
not something that is published. I know of at least two times this has
happened, including the case above and another one that was featured on
"American Greed." Like Bitran and son, another large hedge fund (which
had turned into a Ponzi scheme) was trying to get out of its own mess.
The hedge fund manager was out of money and, in effect, put it all on the
roulette wheel for one last shot. He also lost and ended up in jail.

The SEC is not perfect, and can't be everywhere at all times. But let's
go over it again. ***There are no secrets, there is no quicker way, and there***
is no more sophisticated way. There is just patience and time. There is a
miracle here. It is the miracle of capitalism and free markets and human
innovation. It is going on around you every day. We live during an
amazing time, when you can invest in the great companies of the world
for a $7 commission. We don't have to do all the work and innovation; we
just have to be smart and take what the market offers us every day.

What if something new comes up or someone cracks the code on
how to make money? It won't happen, because short-term moves are

random. As pattern seekers, we want desperately to believe that we can predict the future. We look for past patterns to guess outcomes. For instance, many people are highly influenced (most often in gambling) by the concept that they are *due to win*. They believe if they flip heads 20 times in a row, they are now due to flip tails. Of course, the odds are exactly the same as on the first flip: 50–50. Each flip is called an *independent trial*. It is both funny and sad to watch a 75-year-old woman with her arms wrapped around a slot machine as she sends her husband for more change. She has been playing and losing for so long that she reasons the machine has to be due. This is a classic example of magical thinking.

What if something new comes up or
someone cracks the code on how to make money?
It won't happen, because short-term moves are random.

As much as we would like to think intelligent people can't believe wrong and strange things, they can and do all the time. For example, 40% of people—including some very smart ones I know personally—believe that psychics have worked with police and the FBI to solve crimes. In fact, there has never been a documented case of a psychic solving a crime, and two-thirds of police departments have policies against using psychics. When they are used, it is at the request of the family—and many times, they interfere with investigations. The police may use a psychic if they have a suspect who is prone to believe in psychics, just to make the suspect nervous. The fact that psychics don't solve crimes seems to have no effect on that industry as a whole. The psychics themselves really do believe they have solved the crime, but the police "just wouldn't listen."

Again, you can't reason someone out of something they weren't reasoned into in the first place. The belief in psychic phenomena comes about the same way as all false beliefs. The believer sees it work by coincidence a few times and becomes convinced there is a *pattern*. We will explore this more in Section 3, but for now, as we talk about technical analysis, we are talking about the same pattern-seeking behavior that leads people to believe it works. For our purposes, I will use the term technical analysis to mean any type of investment strategy that uses charts, signals, patterns, up and down trends, moving averages, etc. This includes any method that purports to know the future behavior from past random events.

My overall thesis is that these techniques have come about largely because we feel better if we are doing something rather than nothing. Constant trading gives people something to do, and gives some the illusion of sophistication and special knowledge. The best argument to convince you that this stuff doesn't work is that there are no examples of it working. Think about this: If someone had a secret pattern that could help them pick winners and time the movements of the market, they would be very wealthy. That's hasn't happened. Also, if you had a secret way of using technical analysis that could produce outsized returns, someone would be using it to manage a mutual fund or other pooled account. When they do use it, the results are horrible.

I have watched a long list of timing-based managers go under in the past 30 years. The first timing mutual funds I was pitched were called "Right Time Funds." They never achieved good returns and went out of business within five years.

Magical Thinking in Technical Analysis

If you came into my office and gave me $1 million to invest, and I said I would invest it but I want to wait until my candlestick pattern forms a Gravestone Doji, you would (and should) run for the exits. But this stuff happens every day. They just don't talk about it, for obvious reasons. The technical analysis guys would say I just don't "get it." Oh, I get it. I just don't believe in it.

Technical analysis is truly a belief system, very much like astrology and tarot cards. As humans, we seek patterns even when we don't think we are. I am a fisherman, and I have literally thousands of flies and lures in my boxes. Inevitably, I use the ones that I think are hot. The bite was hot when I had those lures tied on, but my brain tells me it's the lure. I have lures that I have never caught fish on, mostly because I don't use them. And when I think back, I realize I probably tried them when a stick of dynamite could not have produced a fish. I sought a pattern when there was none.

Below are some of the names from the strange world of technical analysis. (Also see Appendix 4.)

Candlestick Patterns:

- Bullish/Bearish Belt Hold
- Bullish/Bearish Engulfing
- Piercing line/Dark Cloud Cover
- Morning Star/Evening Star
- Hammer/Hanging Man
- Doji
- Gravestone Doji/Dragon Fly Doji
- Shooting Star
- Long Legged Doji
- Doji Star
- Harami

Chapter 6 Takeaways:

1. Think of some patterns/habits you have that may have started due to false information.

2. Fakes are pitched every day in all types of media. Quack cures and investments lead the list. Gold has been the top advertisement for the last several years.

3. What is the difference between a trader and an investor?

4. We are pattern seekers. Always be aware of how you do this to yourself.

Before You Leave Section 1...

Obviously, I have some strong opinions on how investing works—and more importantly, how it doesn't work. All that noise you hear out there is mostly nonsense. I have not come to these conclusions easily, but through a significant commitment of time and money and sweat. I believe them to be as true as anything can be. Before we proceed to Section 2, a caveat: I have tried to give you *proof* that this is the right information. I know from every study I have seen and from every experience I have had that proof won't convince a made-up mind.

If you are bound and determined to involve magical thinking in your finances, I can't stop you. I do believe, however, that you will fail. How do I know that? When you go to buy the $200 million Powerball ticket I may say, "You will never win." Technically, I know that you could win. But for all practical purposes, you won't. If you try to build wealth for yourself and your family or the causes you care about by playing the lottery, your odds of success will be the same as if you believe in the easier way or the secret way to invest. You will be putting yourself on the side of the many who fail, versus the few who have the wisdom to succeed.

You need to know going in that you really can't lose if you buy quality assets and hang on for 15–20 years or more. You have to know what your rewards are for the price you will pay. Remember that the only price you will pay for growth is patience. The patience can be hard or easy. But the faith and patience you use is based on fact, not on gimmicks and scams. Good companies and real estate will become more valuable. That is a fact. The only variable is your behavior. I can't send you to the moon for 15 years and then have you come back and look at your portfolio. You must keep your brain away from your money. That can be done, and is a lot easier and more practical than the moon trip.

Stay away from the news, because it is mostly not news but commentary. We have built a cult of people who truly believe they can predict the short-term future. They can't, but we can all predict the future over the longer haul. You can predict that your grandkids will cost more money to raise than your kids. You know Motel 6 used to cost $6 a night; now it's $50, and in 15 years or so, it will rise to $100. Those aren't the types of predictions you get on financial media.

If you're interested in furthering your understanding of these principles, take 15–30 minutes and search for "market outlook" for 2009, 2010, 2011, etc. See if those articles provided any helpful predictive power when they were printed.

Let me leave you with one of my favorite quotes:

"Thousands of experts study overbought indicators, oversold indicators, head-and-shoulder patterns, put-call ratios, the Fed's policy on money supply, foreign investment, the movement of the constellations through the heavens, and the moss on oak trees, and they can't predict markets with any useful consistency, any more than the gizzard squeezers could tell the Roman emperors when the Huns would attack."

—Peter Lynch

SECTION 2:
FRAMING THE PROBLEM:
WHAT SHOULD INVESTORS
CONCENTRATE ON?

Verdi Wealth Planning's philosophy has evolved a lot over the years, but some aspects—such as using good judgment—don't change. An important element of that is getting our clients to focus on what we call *the majors*. What qualifies as *major* or *minor* in my view may surprise you, because you haven't heard this concept on TV or in other media. For instance, picking the right financial advisor is major and heavily weighted. (If you blow this one, the rest won't help you.) I have hired many advisors over the years, and am professionally acquainted with many more. The qualifications I consider, however, may be completely different than you would guess.

It is uncomfortable to know that there are really bad advisors out there, but that's the fact. Most of them are honest, or at least think they are. A small minority set out to be crooks—and, unfortunately, sometimes they are the most likeable. We tend to think that professionals are all good, but it isn't so. CPAs, attorneys, and doctors all come in flavors ranging from great, good, and fair to bad, incompetent, and downright scary. That holds true for financial advisors, as well. You need to move carefully and get a referral.

If you spend a few minutes on the comments section at financial websites, you would think that there is a large group of people out there who do well on their own. In addition, many of those commenters enjoy making you feel like you're an idiot if you hire an advisor. I have doubts, though, that the truly financially independent are sitting around commenting on Yahoo message boards—and you shouldn't let some anonymous person shame you into using or not using a personal advisor. You need to do what's right for you in your situation.

A prime reason for seeking out professional advice is because without it, you sooner or later will second-guess yourself. It is inevitable. The right partner, offering steady counsel, will benefit you greatly.

Another item: Our firm stresses unwavering attention to the right things, most importantly the growth of future income. We call this *purchasing power,* and it really is the factor that matters most when you need to replace the income you had during your working years. To accomplish that, you need to focus on behavior; a good advisor can be measured by how well they can get you to react. I would argue, in fact, that picking investments is the easiest work an advisor does. Shifting your concentration to purchasing power, versus the amount of your principal, is hard to pull off. This is an essential mindset for the wealthy.

Eventually, your advisor must retire or pass away. As a result, one of the most important things an older advisor can do is smooth the path for clients to work with the next in line. As a client, you should expect someone who is not only top-notch from a financial-planning perspective, but also brimming with new ideas and energy. I ask people if they really want to work with an advisor *who is unable to retire after 30 years.* To me that is like hiring a lawyer who is in jail! (Note: I've been at this more than 30 years, but I'm still doing it because I love it!)

This section begins with some financial basics. I'll also discuss dividends, how they work, and why they are so important. There is a brief chapter on the types of assets that I believe you should hold in your portfolio. Above all, our firm believes in equity assets and rising income streams—and my goal here is to point you in the right direction.

To find out more, you can always contact
Verdi Wealth Planning directly. We are able to be licensed in
all states, and would be happy if we could help you achieve
your financial dreams. You can visit us or ask us questions
online at www.verdiwealthplanning.com/questions,
or give us a call at (208) 331-7858.

CHAPTER 7

Some Quick Basics

"Financial peace isn't the acquisition of stuff.
It's learning to live on less than you make,
so you can give money back and have money to invest.
You can't win until you do this."

—Dave Ramsey

Whether you're starting out on the wealth-creation path and are serious about making the right moves or you are a veteran investor, there are certain basic principles that you need to apply to have a secure financial future. The main thing I advise people, especially younger ones, is to make sure they "act their wage." Unless you know you've got a limited time to live, postponing gratification is one of the greatest strengths you can have—and you can have it for free.

Build an Emergency Fund

This is an essential step. Having sufficient liquid cash available gives us the courage and ability to invest the rest of our money in real investments, not savings accounts at the bank. You need cash for all kinds of repairs and any other unexpected events you must fund. (The furnace blows up, you have medical expenses that are uncovered, and the car poops out—sometimes all at the same time.) You don't want this stuff on credit cards, and you certainly don't want to pull out of your investments. Nothing makes me cringe more than people taking money out of retirement accounts for emergencies and losing up to half in penalties and taxes. Make up your mind in advance what constitutes an emergency and what doesn't. *Emergency* is a strong word, so keep it one.

There is no rule of thumb for how much an emergency fund should contain. Six months' worth of living income is a common suggestion, but this may too little or too much. If you have stable income, you need less. If you are starting a business, you may need a lot more. Once your money goes into investments, it should stay there. Remember the old ads for the Black Flag Roach Motel? ("The roaches go in…but they don't come out.") That is how you should think about your investments.

The amount of savings you hold should be sufficient to give the courage to use the rest of your money for long-term investing.

Your investments should only be thought of as a machine that produces income to you. You should never have to redeem shares of stock or mutual funds or other investments to sustain your standard of living. We pound that point into our investors' thinking as much as we can. Obviously, the money belongs to our investors and they are free to do what they want with it. ***But we discourage invading principal at all costs.*** We will do everything we can to make sure our clients live only on the dividends or other distributions from their investments. We want them to live on the gravy not on the potatoes. That is why dividend investing is so critical. (More on that topic in Chapter 11.) Without income, you can't live. We are creatures of income and monthly bills, so we generally focus on monthly not yearly income.

My business partner, John Gottschall, likes to talk about the apple tree. If you have an apple tree, you want to produce a lot of good, healthy apples. When they are ripe, you pick them. If you went out and chopped off a huge branch every time you wanted apples, your tree would die. It is the same with your investments: If you dig into principal, you risk losing that principal. There is a mathematical problem that comes into play here. It is called *sequence of returns* and it can kill your nest egg. Negative sequence of returns is like chopping off a branch. Sequence of returns is explained more fully in chapter 9.

Save First and Control Debt

In addition to having an emergency fund, these are a few of the key behaviors that I've observed in my most successful clients, business associates, family members, and friends:

1. **Live below your means.** Get rid of all credit-card debt and any debt that has purchased depreciating assets, which will kill any chance for wealth. This includes auto loans and the biggest nightmare of all time, the dreaded boat loan. My business partner, Mary Walker, likes to say that "boat" is an acronym for "bust out another thousand." (Disclosure: I have owned boats, so I can attest to that.)

2. **Swallow your pride, and do the math.** Want a new Mercedes or F-150 pickup? Everyone knows a car's value drops thousands of dollars the moment you drive off the lot. A rule of thumb: Your car should cost no more than 20% of your annual income. If you make $60,000 per year, you should drive a $12,000 car (or something cheaper, if possible). If you make $100,000, you can afford a $20,000 car. My son just bought a very nice Honda for $7,000. No one really cares what you drive. *Quit buying things you don't need to impress people you don't even like.*

3. **If you are single, look to date people who are more impressed with your lack of debt and a growing savings account and portfolio than your toys.** Avoid the suitor with an apartment and a $50,000 car with a $49,000 loan—which puts them one layoff away from making that nice car a nice *used* car for someone at maybe $35,000. Now, I know you can't pick up someone for a date in a beat-up sedan and yell out, "Hey, but I don't have debt, I own a house, and my stock portfolio pays dividends and is growing!" The right person will figure it out. Be a quality person when it comes to finances. It will show.

4. **The only debt you should carry is a reasonable mortgage.** What is reasonable? Here is my answer: The house you live in should be no more than 2.5 times your annual earnings, and you should always put at least 20% down. Example: If you earn $60,000 per

year, the maximum price for your house should be under $60,000 x 2.5=$150,000. If you put down 20%, you'll have a mortgage of $120,000. That results in a monthly payment (at a 4.5% interest rate) of around $610 per month, plus insurance, taxes, and HOA dues, which will bring your payment up to $800-$1,000 per month.

5. **Give to charity.** There is something about giving that increases our ability to save. I don't know why, but giving does a lot of positive things.

Rent for a While

I've addressed it above, but let's dig a little deeper on homeownership. If you are starting out, you will have friends and relatives yelling at you, "Buy a house, don't throw money away on rent!" Well, renting can be far smarter than buying and being house poor. A house will cost you more than you expect. When you rent and something breaks, it is not your problem—and something will break. In 2009, the country had tens of thousands of homeowners who were one hot-water tank away from foreclosure. And keep in mind, you can't take a tax deduction for mortgage interest if you don't itemize.

If you are renting and an obnoxious neighbor moves in, you can move out. If you own it, you are stuck. You had better enjoy where your house is, because you are likely to live there for a long time.

When you do buy a house, do so for the right reasons. It's not always a great investment in the sense that stocks and bonds are, and, since you live there, it's highly illiquid. The right reasons to buy are:

- The pride of owning the home.
- Your status as a homeowner for job interviews, loan applications, etc.
- You want to stay put and be stable when you raise kids.
- You want and can afford to customize it to your wants and needs.

If you buy, it can make sense to purchase a new or almost-new home unless you are handy or know exactly what you're getting into. An older home, even if updated, has the potential of bleeding you dry over time. I have an older home and I know what updating costs: We have put more into our house in renovations than we paid for it! (We call that "bronzing a turd." I don't mind telling you that since I am a classic turd bronzer.) On the positive side, we love our home, it is paid off, and it is nice.

Property taxes and homeowner's association fees can also eat you alive. If you have a 30-year mortgage, be prepared to pay more in property tax in 30 years than your house payment was when you moved in!

Two Unknown Landmines that Can Break You

Of course, the biggest reason for people failing to become wealthy follows a pattern: lack of discipline, not investing consistently, and then making mental mistakes. But what about those who've done all the right things, accumulated a lot of wealth, and are counting the days to retirement? There are still two major risks. (Warning: tough medicine ahead.)

The number-one reason a good retirement gets derailed is divorce. Getting divorced can smash your nest egg. When people split, they have to start new households. Each party loses roughly half of their assets. You can't control what a spouse may do, but if you can work together and stay together, it will save you from the big disaster. So, invest in your marriage and in your spouse. How to do that is beyond the scope of this book, but you can look it up.

The second big landmine is one or more children who drain you of all your money. I am not talking about a child with special needs, because there may be financial help available for that. It's the child who gets into legal trouble, needs ongoing drug treatment, or who makes disastrous financial mistakes. This is heart-wrenching for parents. How can you say no to your own children when they are in serious trouble? Only you can answer this. Financial help from parents, in many cases, becomes enabling more than assistance. It keeps the problem alive. Again, I wouldn't dare offer too much advice here, because it is not my field of expertise. But I know enough to recommend that you foster a culture of self-sufficiency in your family. I would talk early and often that, when the kids are adults, they will be loved, but they will not be bailed out of financial trouble. As they get older and head off to college, you need to set boundaries on what you will and won't pay for—and then stick to them. Whether you pay money to problem kids or don't, you need to be ready for a lot of pain. But it really is important to make a firm stance on this. The child may respect you more for sticking to your guns. At any rate, it's a terrible problem that looms over a lot of families, and it breaks my heart when I see them get torn apart over it.

CHAPTER 8

A New Take on Choosing an Advisor: Financial Advisors Demystified

"The choice to make good choices is the best choice you can choose. Fail to make that choice and on most choices you will lose."

—Ryan Lilly

If you decide to work with an advisor, you need to choose carefully—just don't be so careful that you never choose one, at all. Ultimately, when a client does business with our firm, it is because they decide we are trustworthy and they like us. That may sound too simple, but that is how you will probably make your decision, too. The best way to find a trustworthy advisor is from a trusted referral. It is a great advantage to be referred by someone who has been with an advisor for many years and whose plan is working well.

There is a lot of news and information out there on how to choose a financial advisor. Typically, the general public is told to ask questions about items such as fee levels, specific investment strategies, performance, and opinions on future performance. But performance is an illusion. The only performance that counts is within your own account, and each account we manage is different. It would be irrelevant and unethical to quote specific returns, and, if a prospective advisor does so, you should be cautious. He may be cherry-picking one client's return and quoting that to you. She may say they use models, but those returns would not be accurate because everyone starts, adds, and withdraws at different times. So, please be careful if you hear this type of persuasion. With the exception of pooled funds, there is no way an advisor could quote you returns, and any claims should be audited by an outside source. In practical terms, if an advisor quotes you returns, that is not a good sign.

Education and Experience

A lot of attention is also given to the education and experience of an advisor. My opinion is that both are overrated and tricky to assess. I am a CFP (Certified Financial Planner) with 30 years of experience and six different licenses. That could be good or bad. The CFP board has done a good job of showing why it is a good thing to be a CFP. It is solid, rigorous training, and usually takes a couple of years to complete, but can be done in six months if you are in a big hurry. The board has recently added the requirement to have a bachelor's degree before you take the CFP exam. (That is probably a good thing, although I would argue that some undergraduate degrees aren't acceptable preparation for CFP-hood.) In short, a CFP is a good starting point, not a finishing point.

In a similar vein, making sure your taxes are done by a CPA is a prudent move. Again, the title doesn't include a guarantee of honesty or competence, just an ability to pass the exam. You still need to do your due diligence.

There is also a dark side of the CFP designation: Some companies are now requiring it for salespeople who want to hide behind the CFP badge as a way to sell insurance or other questionable products. That insurance is usually whole-life insurance, which in my view is almost always unnecessary.

Methods of Delivery

There are basically five different methods of delivering financial services or investments to the public:

1. Wire houses
2. Registered investment advisors (RIAs)
3. Independents/hybrids
4. Do-it-yourself/discount broker-dealers
5. Bank reps/insurance companies

Wire houses: These are the companies that are household names, such as Dean Witter, E.F. Hutton, Shearson Lehman Brothers, and Merrill Lynch. Wire houses operating today include J.P Morgan, UBS, and Merrill Lynch (after being bailed out by Bank of America). In addition to name recognition, the other common elements among these behemoths is that they have all either gone through, or are in, bankruptcy, or got bailed out by the government or have been taken over. The wire houses were supposed to be as wholesome as baseball and apple pie, but the past 20 years have proven otherwise.

Wire house brokers are *employees*. Their offices and staff are paid for by the company, as are their advertising and overhead. This can be an advantage for the brokers, in the respect that they can concentrate on serving clients. In addition, the sheer size and resources of these companies give them clout and the access to do underwriting for new stock and bond issues. There are many more broker-dealers with this model of employer and employee.

As a wire house employee, advisors are incentivized to sell proprietary products. *Proprietary products* are packaged investments such as mutual funds that are owned by the same company the broker works for. This creates a potential conflict of interest in selecting investments.

RIAs: These advisors are licensed to work only on a fee basis; they do not earn commissions. Most of these advisors are good professionals. Some of them have developed a holier-than-thou attitude and like to make an issue of the fact that they are not biased by commissions. Instead, they end up being biased about fees. In many cases, an investor will be better served to pay an up-front commission of 4–5% rather than a 1% fee every year for life.

Independents/hybrids: This channel got started in the 1970s and '80s as an alternative to the conventional broker-dealers. It is the fastest-growing delivery system for investments, and it is where I have spent my entire career. While there are hundreds of these broker-dealers, they are usually not household names. The largest is LPL Financial, a public company with more than 14,000 representatives—who are business owners, not employees. They keep a much higher percentage of fees and commissions because they have to pay all the overhead, salaries, benefits, etc. Many of these firms operate under their own names, as we do with Verdi Wealth Planning, which is affiliated with Commonwealth Financial Network (the largest privately held broker-dealer in the U.S.). Many of these brokers, including Verdi Wealth Planning, are affiliated with RIAs to conduct fee-based business, or they may have their own RIA registration. In the latter case, they are referred to as *hybrid advisors.*

I believe this channel of advisors has the most flexibility. There is no need to condemn good commission-based products or ongoing fees, since there is the freedom to do both. Nor is there a temptation to sell house brands, because there are none.

Do-it-yourself/discount broker-dealers: When do-it-yourselfers ask for advice, it's comparable to using LegalZoom.com and then asking your lawyer buddy for help. Online broker-dealers include names such as Ameritrade, Fidelity, Charles Schwab, E*TRADE, etc. Many of them have now started to charge for advice over the phone or in person, so the line is being blurred. While they almost always give you the option of no asset fees and low commissions, you need to watch out for garbage fees with these companies. They can charge you confirmation fees when you trade or may charge inactivity fees if you don't make enough trades, among a whole list of other possibilities. Check your statements. When an independent firm charges an asset-based fee, such as 1%, there are generally no other hidden costs involved—although not all independents pick up these fees, either. The worst of both worlds is to be charged the asset-based fee and then have nickel-and-dime charges on top.

Bank reps/insurance companies: These entities license a massive amount of brokers. Within the investment community, we used to say these guys were insurance agents with a mutual-fund badge, and I imagine it still applies to many of them. I can't imagine any serious advisor or investor doing business in this channel, but it happens every day. Think about it this way: How could an insurance agent—who is keeping track of your fender-benders and your disability and health insurance—have the time and expertise to give long-term service with investment planning, too? They don't. It is just an add-on to make money.

If you use a bank, you may get a different agent every time you go to the bank, and at the risk of generalizing, they are usually not high-quality or experienced advisors. Another caveat: Some people believe that their funds are safer if their advisor is at a bank. This is not true. It doesn't matter where a licensed rep sits, we are all regulated by broker-dealers and ultimately by the U.S. Securities and Exchange Commission and FINRA. Many bank reps are independents working in the bank channel, and most of their accounts are small or unsophisticated investors.

Which type should you use? My personal opinion is to avoid the insurance and bank channels, which are usually the least experienced and professional of the groups. Any of the other channels will work—keeping in mind, it depends more on the person than the company. As you might guess, my bias is toward independents, since we can do both fee and commission business and choose which one is a better value for you. We tend to be in the business a long time and be CFPs.

Avoid financial planners who do everything that comes their way for money. I would be suspect of any advisor who goes outside of investments. Life insurance is an exception, since having enough of it is a prerequisite for starting to invest. And there is only one claim per policy. If your advisor is bugging you to buy long-term care insurance, health care insurance, auto insurance, minor league baseball tickets, etc., I would head for the exits—particularly if the conversation then turns to investments.

Fees

Despite what you've read or heard, fees are not a major determiner of your success. Don't become that person who, as Oscar Wilde put it, "knows the price of everything and the value of nothing." That being said, there are reasonable and unreasonable fees. Fee-based accounts are also a little tricky. If the underlying holdings have separate management fees, you may have to stack those together to derive the true fees. For instance, an advisor may quote you a 1.25% annual fee. So if you invest $200,000, the fees would be $2,500 per year. If the investments he chooses are mutual funds (which also may charge fees) you have to add those fees to the 1.25%. If the advisor puts you in the Fidelity Contra Fund, for instance, the fee is .85% (charged by Fidelity)—which means your total fees on that position are 2.10%. That is a long way from the standard of 1%.

You should not be paying transaction costs or commissions of any kind when in a fee-based account. Those should be part of the package. Be sure you are not getting hit with "ticket charges" or anything at all besides the flat fees. *Watch the first few statements to make sure no charges show up.* Fees usually run between .50% to 2%, which is usually determined by the size of the account. Be aware of where the discounts start. For example, our firm charges a flat 1% up until a certain amount, above which we charge .50%. In the right situation, fee-based accounts can be beneficial for both parties, since the advisor's and client's goals are aligned. The client in a fee-based count can be assured that, when trades take place, there is no financial interest for the advisor. These accounts are usually discretionary, meaning the advisor can place trades at his discretion.

Though low on the list of importance, fees are something the media constantly talks about. Why is that? One reason is they don't have any other real financial advice to give. If they told you to buy good companies and hold on, they would be out of business. As a result, in the absence of value, price becomes everything for the financial media.

What I have never met, and will never meet, is a 65-year-old couple who've done all the right things and failed because the fees on their mutual funds (or whatever) were too high!

Let me stress that, when I say fees are low in importance, this is why: I have met thousands of people who have failed to become wealthy from saving too little, or not having enough in equities, or making dumb decisions because of fear and greed. What I have never met, and never will meet, is a 65-year-old couple who've done the all the right things and failed because the fees on their mutual funds (or whatever) were too high! They might retire with much less than they could have, but if they save regularly, don't panic, and invest in long-term equity assets, they will still be successful—and they will have outperformed 90% of the populace. And they will have gotten a lot of help along the way if they chose the right advisor.

Go back and look at any equity mutual fund that has survived for 30 years. There is not one, including fees, in which the investor would have failed. It is only behavior that can wreck your ship. When the media and advertisements start touting low fees, they are selling their own solution in which they make plenty of money. They usually just cut out the service and the help you would get with fee-based or load funds.

Beware of the Fortune-Tellers

I am leery of anyone who has a strong opinion about where the overall economy is headed in the short term, and you should apply that principle to prospective advisors. The fact is, no one knows. Opinions about the short term can make it difficult to embark on a decade's long strategy. As stated earlier, performance is an illusion, and the only performance that counts is your account. In general, we think financial media are asking the wrong questions, and believe the focus should be very different from what is normally discussed in the media and in everyday conversation.

Cherry Pickers, Back Testers, and Window Dressers

Cherry-picking means showing returns from selected clients who have done unusually well, and I've seen advisors or financial representatives use that tactic too many times to count. Some clients will have higher returns. Younger people will generally have higher returns in bull markets, because they will have more growth stocks.

Back-testing is when a representative shows you "what would have happened" if you had used a certain strategy. It has become popular with more powerful computers. Companies feed different formulas and scenarios for the past 20 years (or some other convenient period) into a computer until it spits out amazing returns. Make sure what you're looking at is something that an actual person has been invested in, rather than a picture of *ideal hindsight*.

Window-dressing may be the most disgusting of the three. This practice is usually done for no other reason than to deceive investors, stockholders, and even unaware board members. *Window dressing* means changing the holdings for a mutual fund or recommended list of stocks at the end of the quarter or the end of the year. The changes usually add stocks they *didn't have that did well* for the year or quarter, and remove stocks that they *did have* that did poorly. That way, when you get the annual recommended list, you say, "Hmm...yeah they got some good picks in there"—when the reality is they put them in a week before the document was sent to you! Don't ever pay attention to the recommended list at a broker-dealer. It will be chock-full of stocks that have done well. If you want to know the truth, ask for the recommended list from the year before and see how that has worked out. Another name for window dressing that is commonly used is *burying the evidence.*

What I Think Matters

There are some simple items you should investigate when selecting a person to be responsible for guiding your family's precious resources. Don't focus on what he or she *does* (which is impossible to know) as much as *who* he or she *is*. More is learned by knowing what someone *has done* versus what they *may do* in the future.

The following are a few real-life issues you should look at. Some may sound a little out of the ordinary, but I'm asking you to think differently here. Would you want the steward of your family's resources to:

- Have been sued several times or sued someone else several times (excessive litigation)?
- Have been involved in domestic violence?
- Be behind or delinquent in child support payments?
- Have declared bankruptcy or several bankruptcies?
- Have poor credit?
- Have a substance abuse problem?
- Have 30, 40, or more minor traffic violations?
- Have no formal education?

This is just a partial list. Here are some action items you can immediately take to learn more about your current or prospective advisor:

Background check: There are two websites to check out. The first is the FINRA website (finra.org). FINRA is one of the industry's regulators. By performing a broker search on their site, you can find out a lot about an advisor. When you find the advisor you are looking for, look under "Disclosure Events." You will see either a "Yes" or "No." If it says "Yes," click on the detailed report. If there are more than three or four incidents listed, I would search for another advisor. FINRA also offers Broker Check (brokercheck.finra.org). It is no trivial event when something is reported on FINRA and shows up on Broker Check. In our office, we have four advisors with 55 years of combined experience, but you will not find one event on the Broker Check site. If you see someone who's been in the business for three years with two incidents, that is a lot; I would argue that's too many for an entire career. When interviewing an advisor, I look at these Broker Check Disclosure Events like I look at DUIs. Almost anyone who drinks can get a DUI. It happens. But when two or three occur, it indicates a very serious problem. We want to see a history of learning from mistakes, not repeating them.

Items that get reported include personal bankruptcies, conflicts of interest, criminal suits, civil suits, and arbitration. *Arbitration* is the investment world's equivalent of being sued. The client has claimed damages and he or she has exhausted other avenues of recourse. This could be for fraud, unsuitable investment recommendations, or other actions the broker has been accused of. In a small percentage of cases, the client's claim is truly baseless, so you do need to read the case. The report should say who won in arbitration. If the broker has three or more arbitrations, there is a serious problem. If you're concerned, ask the broker for their side of the arbitration judgment—it is possible to receive a bad ruling. Look for a pattern, though, as multiple reports of similar complaints is definitely a red flag.

In many states, the second place to look up a prospective advisor would be on the State Supreme Court Data Repository website. These sites list almost every infraction someone has made in the state, including lawsuits, criminal activity, and even minor traffic violations. (If there is no online version of this data in your state, the information can be requested by phone or by mail.)

In today's world, there is a lot of information available to the public. You look, you decide. It's not as if the items listed above will keep someone from being a good advisor, but with all else being equal, what is the point of working with an advisor with issues? I have heard the equivalent of "this time is different" when somebody chooses an advisor with a poor history. They think the advisor will change or has been reformed. That is not likely at all. In fact, we use screening processes for potential clients as well, because we don't want to work with someone with a history of excessive legal problems.

Financial Stability: Is your advisor financially sound? Not rich, but sound. Young advisors may not be well-off, but do they have overwhelming debt? Do they live beyond their personal means? Do they have poor credit? Are they behind in their financial obligations? Does their lifestyle (not wealth) reflect the values you have for your own lifestyle?

The first question to ask a prospective advisor is, *"What kind of retirement plan do you have for yourself?"* and/or *"What kind of plan does your company have for its employees?"* If they don't have a plan, I would search elsewhere. If the cobbler's son had no shoes, one would find another cobbler. Second, if applicable, you should ask, *"Do you provide benefits to your employees?"* If employees are not cared for, your account will likely receive the same treatment.

"Could I have a copy of your credit report?" is a third, perfectly valid question. You can get it on the spot. Offer to pay for it if you have to. It could be a tiny price to save you from disaster. Your advisor should have an exemplary credit rating. Why? Outside of the obvious reasons, if he or she is living paycheck to paycheck, behind on bills, saddled with debt, etc., then he or she may get desperate. Through excessive trading, unsuitable investment recommendations, etc., he or she may use your account to make quick money on high commissions or fees, which is not in your best interests.

If Your Advisor Dies, Leaves, or Gets Fired, What Happens?

If your trusted advisor disappeared tomorrow, what would happen to your assets? In most firms without a succession plan:

- Your assets would revert to the home office. You would have an 800 number to call for any service matters.
- You would be assigned to another advisor.

The new advisor knows nothing about your goals, family, business, values, etc. If your former advisor was doing a good job, this would be a disaster. You have no idea if your new advisor is competent, honest, or reliable.

This is the same situation for your investment professional, your CPA, and in some cases, your attorney. Those people are your team. They need to be there when important life events happen. Death, divorce, illness, or a financial crisis requires attention *now* by someone who knows you and cares about what happens to you.

When you place your trust in an advisor and their firm, you might not think to ask, "How long will your services be available?"

When you are younger—say, under 55—you have the time and energy to switch your team of advisors as needed. As you get older, 65 and up, it is crucial to get set with a team that will get you through to your goals for retirement and beyond. The last thing you want is to have all of your team retire, die, or get fired when you are 80 or 90.

In most cases, kids are not capable or willing to help parents with finances when they get older. And that's OK, because you probably don't want to put that responsibility on family. You need a trusted permanent team that you have complete trust in. If you can't find that team, you are going to have a stressful road with financial matters as you advance in age. This is a time in life when we should be able to relax and spend time on issues that add significance to our lives. Watching CNBC every day and worrying about your money won't add significance.

Do you know how old your CPA is, or your CFP? Many times I find that people are working with advisors who are in their 60s or older with no succession plan of any kind.

In conclusion, I believe you should start by finding out more about the type of person your prospective or current advisor is. Performing due diligence on their regulatory history, criminal background, and financial standing are all important when choosing someone to trust with your family's assets. Once you are comfortable with the knowledge you have gained, then focus your attention on their specific advice. That final component is obviously extremely important, but should be scrutinized only after the major vetting has been done—and you have found someone that you can trust and that you like to be around.

The Intangibles

There are financial planners and there are money managers. Good financial planners will give you much more advice than simply picking investments. A good planner will know all the tricks to maximize your IRAs and other retirement plans. In some cases, they will know the rules better than your CPA. They will explain why it is not wise to take a gain or loss on a position. They will take advantage of losses that can be used to save taxes when available.

A good firm will make sure you have accurate reporting. You should have online access to your accounts and be able to know how much you have invested and what the rate of return has been on your portfolio. It is amazing how many people we meet that have no idea what they have made or lost.

An advisor should know how to handle charitable contributions and when they are deductible and when they are not. They should know that gifting appreciated stock is a great way to give, and be able to recommend the best stocks to give. They understand short-term vs. long-term gains, the tax status of the investments you are in, and are able to do a tax estimate for your portfolio late in the calendar or fiscal year.

The death of a spouse or family member is a particularly critical time to have a skilled advisor, because the nature of the inheritance and the handling of the tax consequences are essential to get right. A truly valuable advisor will have grown to know your family and where the assets should be distributed. In most cases, our office ends up becoming the de facto executor of the estate. We end up making sure the money is distributed to the correct parties and all the rules are followed. We also make sure that your accounts are titled in such a way that you have the easiest time possible in probate or avoid probate all together.

In contrast, a money manager wants to show you a track record, which is always questionable, and send you on your way. You may as well be a do-it-yourself investor, in my opinion. Picking the investments is the fun and easy part. The upkeep is the hard part. You may enjoy planting flowers, but probably not pulling weeds, fertilizing, and watering. Your advisor should be doing the mundane and tedious work. This work has to be exact. For instance, if you forget to take an adequate amount out of your IRA when you are over age 70 1/2, you are penalized 50%! We make sure that and dozens of other things don't happen.

You want to have an advisor who encourages you to do smart things!

If you are not somewhat nervous about telling your advisor you have to stop investing, or want to sell off holdings because of some news event, you probably have the wrong person. Part of our job is to make sure you stay on track. You should also be a little squeamish about informing a good advisor you are buying something you can't afford, like a Ferrari. We will consistently urge you to save and invest and to make smart decisions with your taxes, debts, and investments. We will keep you out of the traps like bad time-share plans or cash-value life insurance.

How and Why Advisors Get Paid

You may have heard rumblings of the federal government's initiatives to make regulating investment advisors "fairer." Such ideas are well intentioned, but extremely misguided as far as why financial advisors get paid for what we do. The belief among the political class is that, if we make the rules "fair," everyone will start maxing out their 401(k) plans and IRAs. At the root of that belief is that lower fees are part of the answer. Here's what is missing: Most 401(k) participants already have huge incentives to save. They get to put money away before tax and a lot of them have their investments *matched* by the company. Even with the automatic 100% return that comes with matching, people don't always invest. How in the world do politicians—and many of the financial talking heads parroting the government line—think lowering fund fees a quarter of a point will put people in the mood to invest?

Some advisors don't agree with me on what I am about to say about advisor compensation. They like to believe they get paid for their brilliant selections of investments. Well, here's a dirty little secret: Any sixth-grader with some help on the phone from the call center at the do-it-yourself brokerage can pick adequate investments to be successful. To me, that is about 10% of the battle. Once the person owns the investments is when the trouble begins. Most people will chase returns by putting money in funds that have gone up and taking from those that have gone down. That is a sure recipe for disaster, but the guy at the call center isn't there to talk you out of this fiscally suicidal situation. (By the way, we absolutely expect to pick better investments than the sixth-grader; the point is that he could pick *adequate* investments.)

Any sixth-grader with some help on the phone from the call center at the do-it-yourself brokerage can pick adequate investments to be successful. To me, that is about 10% of the battle.

Many of the people who start out OK will scurry out of equities after the market has crashed. Another horrible move! These counterproductive decisions (and countless others) completely wipe out your advantage of equity investing in the first place. So, how do we help? When you get right down to it, we get paid to hold on to people's ankles and keep them in the boat. I know that may sound easy. It is not. In fact, it is our hardest job. If you think you can avoid costly mistakes and have discipline in all your decisions, you may be OK doing it yourself. You also have to be ready to do the intangibles listed above, which are also tougher than they look. Keep in mind that what is confusing at age 65 is mind-boggling at 85. You better have someone who is good and trustworthy on your side. If you think a relative can do it, you are most likely in for a disaster—and the survivors are in for some real lousy Thanksgiving dinners.

> *When you get right down to it, we get paid to hold on to*
> *people's ankles and keep them in the boat. I know that may sound easy.*
> *It is not. In fact, it is our hardest job.*

If you think I am just trying to scare you, you are absolutely right. If I or someone else doesn't scare you about all the land mines out there, you will surely step on one.

Everyone pays for financial advice. The amount you pay to an advisor can be peanuts, however, compared to trial and error. How would I know that? Because the problem with advisors and do-it-yourselfers is no one starts out knowing much and it's *costly*. The good news is that when you start out you are playing with smaller stakes and so it won't hurt as much. The real damage comes to people who inherit or earn large amounts of money, like young professional athletes. They pretty much *have* to get advice and it (as you read about often) can be very costly.

Chapter 8 Takeaways:

1. The character of your advisor trumps experience.

2. Don't be afraid to investigate the potential advisor and ask for documents such as credit reports, FINRA documents, and whatever else you need.

3. People don't fail to retire due to high fees. High fees are bad, but won't keep you from being successful if you're doing everything else right.

4. As advisors, we earn our money by keeping people on track and doing the intangibles for them that they don't know about.

5. Picking investments is about 10% of the battle. After that, you have to go to work on your brain.

6. Your advisor should encourage you to invest consistently and not panic. A good advisor will hold on to your ankles and keep you in the boat.

7. Make sure you like your advisor or you will be in for a rough time.

Mindful Money Questions:

1. What is window dressing?

2. What is cherry-picking?

3. What is back-testing?

4. How many more years will your advisors be there to help you?

5. Do they have a succession plan—and if so, what is it?

CHAPTER 9

Purchasing Power:
The Only Thing that Matters

Purchasing Power, also called buying power. The ability to purchase goods and services. The value of money in terms of what it can buy at a specified time compared to what it could buy at some period established as a base: The purchasing power of the dollar.

—Investopedia

"In fact, for someone in the highest tax bracket, short-term Treasury bills have yielded a negative after-tax real return since 1871, even lower if state and local taxes are taken into account. In contrast, top-bracket taxable investors would have increased their purchasing power in stocks 288-fold over the same period."

—Jeremy J. Siegel, *Stocks for the Long Run 5/E: The Definitive Guide to Financial Market Returns & Long-Term Investment Strategies*

I believe purchasing power is the most important concept you can learn as you try to attain wealth. It's not just about staying ahead of inflation, even though that is the most important part. Many times, the concept of purchasing power is what keeps people in the markets long enough to actually get where they need to be.

When setting goals for a retirement income plan, many industry professionals, and subsequently their clients, tend to focus on the irrelevant. The irrelevant is almost always the focus on what the current principal amount of an investment portfolio is worth, and a constant obsession with avoiding losses and pleasing clients in the short run.

That, in my opinion, is irrelevant unless immediate or very short-term liquidity is needed. This focus almost always includes a number (principal amount of assets saved) somewhere distant in the future, and projections on how efficiently one can get to that number. You've even probably heard the phrase, "What's your number?"

We have addressed inflation, which is the number-two culprit in underperformance behind fear and greed. The odd concept of building up a mountain of money and then fretfully drawing it down is not what you had pictured for retirement. The big pile of money is good. It's the fretting we want to avoid.

I have looked a 93-year-old man in the eye who had so much money that he could put it in a vault, draw out $5,000 a day, and would have to live to 150 to run out of money. His number-one fear? Running out of money. You don't get immune to it; you train yourself out of it in the first place. That's a process that requires facts, history, and faith. Faith that the sun is going to come up tomorrow and go down tomorrow night. The fact that we have lived through some hard times and atrocities. We have seen nations collapse. And whatever is causing you to worry about your money at the moment, remember: This too shall pass. In six weeks or six months, your worry will move seamlessly to another crisis du jour—which also will pass.

The odd concept of building up a mountain of money and then fretfully drawing it down is not what you had pictured for retirement.

Most important is to realize that purchasing power is much different from your pile of money. Your pile will go up and down. In the long run, it will go up. Remember, quality equity assets get more valuable over time—and this time is not different. Remember the disconnect between stock prices and the underlying earnings and dividend growth? Let's go back and use Exxon as an example. We want to be loaded up with stocks and real estate that have proven over many decades that they are capable of rising dividends and rents. There are a lot of companies like that. Exxon has raised its dividend every year for 33 years. It becomes corporate culture to distribute cash and increase the dividend payment.

Let's say, for example, that you come into my office and purchase $1 million worth of Exxon stock. (We are assuming you have a lot of other diversification). Next, let's say the current dividend on Exxon is 3.5% and the share price is $100, just for the sake of easy math. This is how it looks on our Purchasing Power Report:

Holding	Value	Yield	Annual Income	Monthly Income
XOM	$1,000,000	3.5%	$35,000	$2,943

If I am retired, I know I won't invade principal. I have already made that decision. I know that I will receive about $3,000 per month from my Exxon stock. Now, let's say we meet annually. When you come in at the end of one year, your Exxon stock has gone down 20% and is now worth $800,000. That is not good. I don't expect you to do backflips in the office due to excitement. But in reality, it is not bad. What does your Purchasing Power Report now look like? What is your dividend yield as a percentage? What is your monthly income? I ask a lot of people these questions. The most frequent answer would be that the dividend and yield are both down 20%, just like the stock. But that's not true. Your new report would look something like this:

Holding	Value	Yield	Annual Income	Monthly Income
XOM	$800,000	4.8%	$37,246	$3,127

As you can see, your monthly income has increased. When you walk out to the mailbox to get your check, it will be larger that it has been. How can that be? Because your yield is inversely related to price. Also, Exxon continued their policy of raising dividends each year *per share.*

It is confusing at first. Let's use another example, this time in real estate. You buy a rental home for $100,000, and receive monthly rent of $833.33. It would look like this:

House Value	Rent/Monthly Income	Annual Rent	Income Yield
$100,000	$833	$10,000	10%

In the next year, two things have happened. One, the prices of houses has dropped. Rental rates are up, however, and you built in a 2% increase as the landlord. Let's say your house is now worth $80,000. Depressing? Not really, assuming you have good tenants. What is your yield now? What is the monthly income? This is how your rental statement would look:

House Value	Rent/Monthly Income	Annual Rent	Income Yield
$80,000	$866.67	$10,000	12%

See how that works? The house has gone down in price, making the rent a higher percentage in terms of yield.

Your yield looks like this:

Year 1 $10,000/$100,000   =   10% yield
Year 2 $80,000/$10,000   =   12% yield

Notice that you also got a raise in your income. Again, assuming good property and good tenants, do you have to fret that the principal has gone down? Do you know that in 20 years the house will be worth considerably more? Of course it will. How do you know this? One more time: Quality equity assets get more valuable over time. And, this time it's not different.

As a retiree or retiree candidate, this just means that you have increased your income and can buy as many hamburgers this year as you did last year.

Where Is the Focus?

Each client gets a Purchasing Power Report from us each quarter or semi-annually. The form looks like this:

Verdi Wealth Planning Holdings

Account	Investment		Value	Distribution Rate/Current Yield	Annual Income			Monthly Income			Income Taken
John Roth IRA	CASH	$	395.62	0.00%	$	-	$	-	$		-
	ACME FUND	$	34,000.00	4.56%	$	1,550.40	$	129.20	$		-
	ACME FUND	$	7,646.57	3.91%	$	298.98	$	24.92	$		-
John Roth IRA Total		$	42,042.19	4.40%	$	1,849.38	$	154.12	$		-
John IRA	CASH	$	13,000.00	0.00%	$	-	$	-	$		-
	ACME FUND	$	89,500.00	2.56%	$	2,291.20	$	190.93	$		-
	ACME FUND	$	66,400.00	3.25%	$	2,158.00	$	179.83	$		-
	ACME FUND	$	53,200.00	2.12%	$	1,127.84	$	93.99	$		-
	ACME FUND	$	98,780.00	4.30%	$	4,247.54	$	353.96	$		-
	ACME FUND	$	23,400.00	3.10%	$	725.40	$	60.45	$		-
John IRA Total		$	344,280.00	3.06%	$	10,549.98	$	879.17	$		-
Jane Roth IRA	CASH	$	4,107.43	0.00%	$	-	$	-	$		-
	ACME FUND	$	27,309.99	4.30%	$	1,174.33	$	97.86	$		-
	ACME FUND	$	10,990.25	4.94%	$	542.92	$	45.24	$		-
Jane Roth IRA Total		$	42,407.67	4.05%	$	1,717.25	$	143.10			
Jane IRA	Cash	$	7,054.82	0.00%	$	-	$	-	$		-
	ACME FUND	$	86,700.00	2.23%	$	1,933.41	$	161.12	$		-
	ACME FUND	$	21,847.57	3.67%	$	801.81	$	66.82	$		-
	ACME FUND	$	19,538.00	7.00%	$	1,367.66	$	113.97	$		-
	ACME FUND	$	25,647.00	3.10%	$	795.06	$	66.25	$		-
	ACME FUND	$	17,854.00	5.19%	$	926.62	$	77.22	$		-
	ACME FUND	$	18,331.95	6.01%	$	1,101.75	$	91.81	$		-
Jane IRA Total		$	196,973.34	3.52%	$	6,926.31	$	577.19			
Joint TOD	Cash	$	925.84	0.00%	$	-	$	-	$		-
	ACME FUND	$	37,538.23	6.91%	$	2,593.89	$	216.16	$		-
Joint TOD Total		$	38,464.07	6.74%	$	2,593.89	$	216.16			
TOTALS		$	664,167.27	3.56%	$	23,636.81	$	1,969.73	$		-

Growth of Purchasing Power vs. CPI

Year		2014	2015	2016	2017	2018
Annual Purchasing Power (PP)¹	$	21,545.00 $	22,334.80 $	23,636.81		
Purchasing Power Growth YTD		5.20%	3.67%	5.83%		
CPI Increase YTD		1.32%	0.50%	1.69%		

Purchasing Power

As of 01/25/2017
John and Jane Doe

412 E PARKCENTER BLVD, SUITE 200 BOISE, ID 83706
208 / 3317058 office 208 / 356-9989 fax

Verdi Wealth Planning Holdings Summary

Below is a representation of the hypothetical income you could draw off of your accounts as of the date of this report. The income taken column represents the actual income you are receiving off of each account.

Account		Value	Distribution Rate/Current Yield	Annual Income		Monthly Income		Income Taken
John Roth IRA Total	$	42,042.19	4.40%	$	1,849.38	$	154.12	$ -
John IRA Total	$	344,280.00	3.06%	$	10,549.98	$	879.17	$ -
Jane Roth IRA Total	$	42,407.67	4.05%	$	1,717.25	$	143.10	$ -
Jane IRA Total	$	196,973.34	3.52%	$	6,926.31	$	577.19	$ -
Joint TOD Total	$	38,464.07	6.74%	$	2,593.89	$	216.16	$ -
TOTALS	$	664,167.27	3.56%	$	23,636.81	$	1,969.73	$ -

Growth of Purchasing Power vs. CPI

This chart tracks the annual % increase of your purchasing power (hypothetical income) vs. the Consumer Price Index (inflation). The goal is to have your current or future income growing at a faster rate than inflation. The Purchasing Power Growth includes additions.

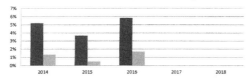

Annual Growth of Purchasing Power

■ Purchasing Power Growth YTD
▨ CPI Increase YTD

verdiwealthplanning.com

Purchasing Power

As of 1/25/2017
John and Jane Doe

412 E PARKCENTER BLVD, SUITE 200 BOISE, ID 83706
208 / 3317058 office 208 / 356-9989 fax

Verdi Wealth Planning Holdings

Account	Investment		Value	Distribution Rate/Current Yield	Annual Income		Monthly Income		Income Taken
John Roth IRA	CASH	$	395.62	0.00%	$ -	$	-	$	-
	ACME FUND	$	34,000.00	4.56%	$	1,550.40	$	129.20	$ -
	ACME FUND	$	7,646.57	3.91%	$	298.98	$	24.92	$ -
John Roth IRA Total		$	42,042.19	4.40%	$	1,849.38	$	154.12	$ -
John IRA	CASH	$	13,000.00	0.00%	$ -	$	-	$	-
	ACME FUND	$	89,500.00	2.56%	$	2,291.20	$	190.93	$ -
	ACME FUND	$	66,400.00	3.25%	$	2,158.00	$	179.83	$ -
	ACME FUND	$	53,200.00	2.12%	$	1,127.84	$	93.99	$ -
	ACME FUND	$	98,780.00	4.30%	$	4,247.54	$	353.96	$ -
	ACME FUND	$	23,400.00	3.10%	$	725.40	$	60.45	$ -
John IRA Total		$	344,280.00	3.06%	$	10,549.98	$	879.17	$ -
Jane Roth IRA	CASH	$	4,107.43	0.00%	$ -	$	-	$	-
	ACME FUND	$	27,309.99	4.30%	$	1,174.33	$	97.86	$ -
	ACME FUND	$	10,990.25	4.94%	$	542.92	$	45.24	$ -
Jane Roth IRA Total		$	42,407.67	4.05%	$	1,717.25	$	143.10	
Jane IRA	Cash	$	7,054.82	0.00%	$ -	$	-	$	-
	ACME FUND	$	86,700.00	2.23%	$	1,933.41	$	161.12	$ -
	ACME FUND	$	21,847.57	3.67%	$	801.81	$	66.82	$ -
	ACME FUND	$	19,538.00	7.00%	$	1,367.66	$	113.97	$ -
	ACME FUND	$	25,647.00	3.10%	$	795.06	$	66.25	$ -
	ACME FUND	$	17,854.00	5.19%	$	926.82	$	77.22	$ -
	ACME FUND	$	18,331.95	6.01%	$	1,101.75	$	91.81	$ -
Jane IRA Total		$	196,973.34	3.52%	$	6,926.31	$	577.19	
Joint TOD	Cash	$	925.84	0.00%	$ -	$	-	$	-
	ACME FUND	$	37,638.23	6.91%	$	2,593.89	$	216.16	$ -
Joint TOD Total		$	38,464.07	6.74%	$	2,593.89	$	216.16	
TOTALS		$	664,167.27	3.56%	$	23,636.81	$	1,969.73	$ -

verdiwealthplanning.com

Purchasing Power

As of 1/25/2017
John and Jane Doe

Growth of Purchasing Power vs. CPI

Year		2014	2015	2016	2017	2018
Annual Purchasing Power (PP)'	$	21,545.00	$ 22,334.80	$ 23,636.81		
Purchasing Power Growth YTD		5.20%	3.67%	5.83%		
CPI Increase YTD		1.32%	0.50%	1.69%		

Purchasing Power

As of 01/25/2017
John and Jane Doe

01.25.2037 - Hypothetical Illustration (Including Outside Holdings)

Below is a representation of your current and/or hypothetical future holdings of your accounts (including outside holdings and/or income sources) utilizing the hypothetical growth rate, annual additions, and future retirement date or other date we have mutually agreed upon.

			Hypothetical Value (12.31.2037)	Hypothetical Distribution Rate/Yield	Hypothetical Annual Income (12.31.2037)	Hypothetical Monthly Income (12.31.2037)
Current Holdings		$	2,340,289.72	5.00% $	117,014.49	$ 9,751.21
Annual Additions	$	40,000.00 $	1,653,958.00	5.00% $	82,697.90	$ 6,891.49
Other?				$	-	$ -
John Soc Sec				$	24,000.00	$ 2,000.00
Jane Soc. Sec.				$	24,000.00	$ 2,000.00
Totals		$	3,994,247.72	$	247,712.39	$ 20,642.70
			6.5% Growth			

What's So Bad About Selling Principal for Income?

*"The order or the sequence of investment returns is a primary concern for those individuals who are retired and living off the income and capital of their investments. It is not just long-term **average** returns that impact your financial wealth, but the timing of those returns. When retirees begin withdrawing money from their investments, the returns during the first few years can have a major impact on their wealth."* —Investopedia

This concept can be confusing, because people with the same amount of money at retirement and who earn the same average annual return over a long period, say 30 years, can have drastically different results. One couple may thrive while the other goes broke. How can this be? It is all because of the choice by investors and advisors to invade principal to provide income! If you are forced to sell shares of stocks and funds when the market is down, you inflict permanent damage to your portfolio. If you just take the income produced, you never reduce the amount of shares—and as the market recovers, your principal may regain its original value or more.

Picture two enormous snowballs that are exactly the same size. They will both sit for 60 days in an *average temperature of 45 degrees*, but in different locations. Which one will melt faster? You want to say they will melt at the same rate, and they may…but only if the temperature is a constant 45 degrees at each location. But look at what happens if that's not the case. One location starts out at 85 degrees for the first 20 days and melts the snowball altogether, before returning to well below freezing for the next 40 days. The other one spends the first 20 days below freezing and the next 40 days just warm enough to bring the average to 45 degrees. Sequence matters: One is a puddle after 20 days, and the other goes the distance.

In the columns below are some very interesting numbers that illustrate the snowball principle in a financial context. We are looking at basically identical couples facing retirement. They are both each 65 years old, have the same amount of money accumulated, and have the same income needs. Which will be more successful? Again, like the snowballs, you tend to think they will fare the same. But they don't.

Why? Because like the temperatures for the snowballs, the returns don't come in the same *sequence* as each other. Let's look at the example below. Both couples have $2 million in retirement and both need $100,000 per year in income. (In reality, they also need an increase of 3% or so per year to keep up with inflation, but we won't include that for simplicity's sake.)

Understanding Sequence-of-Returns (A Hypothetical Illustration)

	YEAR	Portfolio A Return	Portfolio A Balance* $100,000	Portfolio B Return	Portfolio B Balance* $100,000
The combination of the market's impact and the $7,000 yearly withdrawal leaves Portfolio A with less than $76,000 at the end of year one.	1	-18.39%	$75,897	26.57%	$117,710
	2	-19.14%	$55,710	19.61%	$132,420
	3	-4.59%	$46,475	5.26%	$132,017
	4	18.47%	$46,766	16.57%	$145.733
	5	6.79%	$42,466	33.60%	$185,347
	6	14.30%	$40,537	21.23%	$216,210
	7	-15.39%	$28,376	13.92%	$238,332
	8	14.59%	$24,495	-1.61%	$227,608
	9	8.95%	$19,060	21.03%	$267,002
	10	19.52%	$14,414	16.21%	$302,148
	11	20.72%	$8,951	20.72%	$356,303
	12	16.21%	$2,267	19.52%	$417,486
Portfolio A runs out of money by year 13 because of the negative returns it experiences at the outset.	13	21.03%	$0	8.95%	$447,225
	14	-1.611%	$0	14.59%	$504,454
	15	13.92%	$0	-15.39%	$420,896
	16	21.23%	$0	14.30%	$473,083
	17	33.60%	$0	6.79%	$497,730
	18	16.57%	$0	18.47%	$581,367
	19	5.26%	$0	-4.59%	$548,004
	20	19.61%	$0	-19.14%	$437,456
	21	26.57%	$0	-18.39%	$351,295

Source: Fidelity Research Institute, QWeMA Group Inc, Aug 2007.

*Starting balance = $100,000
Withdrawals = $7,000/year

The Purchasing Power statement (pages 105–107) offers perspective on the sequence of returns, listing each position owned and the distribution rate/yield of the underlying investments. This way, the client can always see not only what the lump sum looks like, but how much income the portfolio is producing. More importantly, it shows the gain or loss of purchasing power from year to year. To me, that is the only thing that really matters as I look forward to retirement. As you can see, we graph the growth of purchasing power against the enemy of income, which is inflation. If your income is losing year to year to inflation, you are in trouble. If you start having less income year after year, eventually you will have to invade principal.

The Retirement Dilemma

More than 90% of people we work with want help with retiring. It is the ultimate American goal—even though we may have no idea of what retirement will look like or feel like. What needs will it meet? What needs will be lost? Our firm is very good at getting people from zero to retirement over many time frames. (I don't mean zero dollars, just zero plan or zero chance the way they are headed.) One of the first questions we ask, even to an older client, is "Why do you want to retire? Who invented this concept? How old is it? I don't remember Moses retiring. I don't remember Ben Franklin retiring. They just fell over dead doing what they were good at. It never occurred to them that they had to build the mountain, then grind it down. Why does that occur to you to do it that way?"

We sit with the client to fill out a basic retirement brain jogger. We ask some thinking questions, which many times the client has not heard or thought much about:

- Why do you want to retire?
- How will you spend your time?
- How will your social network change?

Usually we can work with them and slowly help them gain something they have never had, which is a coherent philosophy on how to proceed consistently over time toward their goals.

To perform the right actions for success, you must be thinking the right thoughts. When I interview a potential client, I carefully listen for how the person is thinking. I ask questions that will reveal his or her assumptions about money. After the interview I may say, "She's thinking all the right thoughts," or "He's thinking all the wrong thoughts." If the prospect is thinking the right thoughts, they qualify. If they are thinking the wrong thoughts, it is my job to determine if they are open to change—sometimes radical change—in what they are doing. Usually, we can work with them and slowly help them gain something they have never had, which is a coherent philosophy on how to proceed consistently over time toward their goals.

Broken Dreams: Our Failed Retirement System

When President Franklin Delano Roosevelt signed the Social Security Act of 1935, it was designed to be a safety net for those who had reached the age at which working was not an option. Our laws are usually well intentioned. They are meant to be the means by which we act out the great spiritual and human values we founded the nation on. Caring for our poor and sick was and is a noble goal. Social Security has been a useful tool to make sure that those who can't work can live with some dignity and fully participate in our great country.

But, something happened along the way. Politicians, eager to out-do-good the opposition, have promised more and more with less and less. And like most of our citizens, they have not thought through the long-term implications of their decisions. We could have guessed this, right? A great country gets big, rich, and too sloppy. They lose control of the original initiatives that started as noble causes.

We see the same phenomenon in legendary corporations. Bill Gates no longer controls Microsoft. Microsoft has grown, and as it has grown, control has gone to the many instead of the people who loved the company originally and made things work well. Gates is no longer the benevolent dictator who nurtured the small company at the beginning. He couldn't change its course now if he tried. He now has stockholders, unions, consumer groups, government regulations, and boards of directors.

This is part of the reality that is tough to take as an American. We don't live in the same country as our fathers and grandfathers. We need to not see this as a disaster, however, but as an inevitable consequence of success. The person who is hired on at Microsoft today does not have the same opportunity as the first few employees. It's different. But that's OK. The American dream is not dead. It just moved around and sometimes we can't find it. Meanwhile hundreds of new businesses start each month—even in the depths of recession—and prosper.

We will need to fix the system at some point. Politicians on both sides are paralyzed with fear. They talk about changing Social Security and other entitlements. The biggest voting blocs—i.e., retirees and others on government benefits—do not want to hear anything about cutting benefits. Unfortunately, entitlements make up about 65% of the federal budget. Congress is constantly trying to make cuts in the discretionary part of the budget, but that's only about 12% of the whole enchilada. If your household income is $5,000 per month and your house payment is $5,100, you can't balance the books by cutting down your grocery bill. That is exactly what is going on in Congress.

Soon we will have to adjust the system to meet reality. When President Roosevelt signed the bill, there were about 45 workers paying into Social Security for every person retired. Due to longer lives (a good thing!), we now have only about three people paying in for every one person on Social Security. It won't work. If only Roosevelt had added one more paragraph that read:

"Benefits will adjust according to life expectancy and the ratio of workers to non-workers over time. This will be done by raising the age at which people are able to collect Social Security."

With those two sentences, the government could have slowly raised the age to collect benefits to reflect reality. Of course, that didn't happen. Politicians are like anyone else. They don't see the long run very well. Some of them only see until the next election. It's not necessarily slimy; it's just built into the system.

The retirement age has been raised a tiny bit, but soon they will have to break it to people under 55 or 45 that they have to wait a few years more. Maximum benefits can be collected by a 60-year-old now at age 66. That could stay the same. Someone who is 55, however, may have to wait until 68; a 50-year-old until 69; a 40-year-old until 72, etc. And in reality, today's 72-year-old has a higher quality of life than a 65-year-old had back then. It really is the only solution and I believe we will see this sometime fairly soon.

Would you like a custom Purchasing Power Report?
Contact us at VerdiWealthPlanning.com/purchasingpowerreport

Chapter 9 Takeaways:

1. Yield and price are negatively correlated.
2. As investors, we need to find companies who have an excellent chance of raising dividends and earnings.
3. Focus on purchasing power and not on the pile/lump sum.
4. Inflation is the second-biggest risk you have after behavioral risk.
5. The rate of increase for stocks in the S&P 500 is above long-term inflation.
6. Never invade principal.

Mindful Money Questions:

1. How does the price of your shares affect the dividend payout and earnings?
2. What assets go up over time and have stayed ahead of inflation?

CHAPTER 10

Please, Please Downsize!

"Have nothing in your houses that you do not know to be useful or believe to be beautiful."

—William Morris

"If you don't take our advice, why are you paying us?" In short, that's what we say to investors when they don't take our advice. One of the most common times is when clients resist downsizing and moving when they get to an age when they need simplification and convenience. The decision to downsize your residence as you get older is both financial and emotional. I don't hold the prudence of moving as doctrine or fact, but simply one of observation and common sense.

The average size of a house in 1956 was 958 square feet. Today it is around 2,600 square feet. What are we doing with all that empty space?

At any given time in this business, I have several older clients who are literally stranded in their houses. They cannot drive. Therefore they can't get groceries, go to the doctor, church, etc. If they are lucky, they have family who can bring in supplies and give them rides. (The kids love you, but taking stuff to your house because you are stuck gets old in a hurry and can create a lot of grief in family relations.) If they don't have friends or family to help out, the costs can run into the thousands of dollars per month.

It typically works like this: The kids know the parents should move from the 4,000-square-foot home that is out-of-date and has a basement or an upstairs that must be navigated by increasingly less-mobile parents. In some cases, the house and yard are run down. Money isn't always the issue. The energy and desire it takes to remodel usually lessens as our clients age. Generally, the older people become, the greater the emotional attachment to the house. Sometimes people know they should move for years. But it is too easy not to move. Eventually, it becomes hard, if not impossible, to overcome the inertia.

And it seems to sneak up on us. Years go by, and moving is discussed as something always in the future. At this point, we know that this will most likely end badly. The kids will get a call that someone has had a medical emergency, maybe resulting in a long period of hospitalization or rehabilitation. When they come home, they still need a lot of care. Now it is basically too late to sell and move. The couple becomes stranded. Sometimes one person can drive and be mobile, but they are reluctant to leave the other spouse alone.

The decision is emotional, because we become attached to objects. Even as I contemplate trading in my old truck, I am struck by an emotional attachment to the machine. After all, we have been through so much together. Think of all the good times, all the memories. With a vehicle, this emotion usually wears off for me as soon as "old Betsy" starts nickel-and-diming me to death with repairs. With a house, the attachment is much stronger. Even though the house will eventually nickel-and-dime you to death, too, you will have an overwhelming urge to stay in it. The inertia is always in favor of *not moving*. The older you get, the stronger the inertia gets—and the more important it is to downsize. I have been called heartless in my quest to get clients to downsize, as if a house were a beloved family pet that I was suggesting should be euthanized before its time.

I'm guilty of resistance on the housing front, too. I admit that my original idea was to stay in the house we raised the kids in so they could come home and sleep in their old bedroom and use the old shower. That is all good when the kids are 30 and you are 60 or 70. But when the kids are 50 or 60 and you are 80 or 90, the charms of the "old shower" will wear off very quickly in reality. In most cases, the baby boomers' and GenXers' fear that their parents will become stranded in a huge, out-of-date house far outweighs the sentimental value.

Talk this over with your family. Now. Make a commitment to not get stuck in your house. Remodeling is an option, but it is expensive and can become a nightmare. You are unlikely to get your value back out of the house when you leave. Putting a lot of money into updating a house rarely makes sense. You can spend $200,000 updating a $300,000 house. Despite what the remodeling industry claims, the price of the house will not go up $200,000. As I discussed earlier, you're in danger of bronzing a turd.

The typical baby boomer owns a 2,700-square-foot home, sometimes much larger. If you are living in 3,000 square feet, you can comfortably downsize to 1,500 square feet. Think about the lifestyle you want at age 75 or 80. The house can be designed to be big enough to entertain a dozen or more people. Holidays seem to be high on the list for reasons not to downsize, so I suggest you learn to not feel obligated to cook every year. It can become habit-forming!

Some people are frozen by a fear of change, psychologists say. The prospect of leaving the place that is the center of your universe and a constant in your life can be frightening. Finding a new grocery store can stir up deep emotions. There may also be changes in doctors, dentists, pharmacists, and places of worship. This can become overwhelming at any age, but it only gets worse as you get older.

So what are we to do? My advice is to make a plan and stick with it. If you believe you will be healthy at age 80, then plan to move at age 76 or 77. Pick a date and stick to it. When you are retired, go out and look at houses that would be ideal for you when you are older. Have some fun looking forward to a new house.

Chapter 10 Takeaways:

1. The average size of a house in the U.S. has grown from 958 square feet to over 2,600 square feet. That has happened as family size has shrunk.

2. Decide how much space you really need. You spend 90% of your time in 10% of your house: bed, toilet, shower, TV/computer chair, and a place to sit down for meals.

3. The kids probably don't want to stay over as much as you think they do. They need space and private time.

4. Pick a time three to five years in advance to downsize, and then look forward to it by looking at very nice, new but smaller homes.

5. Stay close to where you need to go the most, i.e., the biking trails, grocery stores, drug stores, doctors' offices, church or synagogue, work, etc.

6. It is very easy to get sentimental over a house. Don't get so sentimental that it hurts your family. In the end, the house is an object full of memories you have projected on it. You gave it the personality it had. That doesn't stay with the house (an object can't do that as much as you want to think it can). Your family members are not objects. They matter. They are the real deal.

7. I have seen a lot of disasters when people stay in the old house too long.

8. What is confusing at 70 is mind-boggling at 90. Simplify.

Mindful Money Questions:

1. What happens when you remodel the old house…and don't move?

2. Do you want to travel?

3. Do you have pets?

4. Can you "lock and walk"?

CHAPTER 11

Dividends, Dividends, Dividends

"That's the gift the keeps on givin'"
—Cousin Eddie, Christmas Vacation

"Do you know the only thing that gives me pleasure? It's to see my dividends coming in."
—John D. Rockefeller, 1901

"If you put together a portfolio of good blue chips, you might start with a yield of 3%. You have to train your brain to ignore the price movement. You want to focus on the income production and the growth of that income."
—Charles Farrell

In general, I love dividends and so do my clients. They truly are the gift that keeps on giving. When I say *dividends*, that includes regular interest payments or any other systematic payment back into your investment produced by the investment itself. This reinvestment grows the amount of shares you own, and since payouts are declared as dollars per share, your dividend keeps going up. There is something very calming about knowing that, if the market goes down, you will be buying cheaper and cheaper shares of the stock or fund.

If your investment does not pay dividends, you just have to wait for the share price to rebound. We call that a *sitting duck*: no dividends means no monthly investments to create dollar-cost-averaging, which is an incredibly powerful tool. Sometimes it will take stocks or real estate 10 or 15 years or more (if at all) to return to their peak from their trough or lowest price. If an investor is receiving regular dividends or rent—and, better yet, growing dividends or rent—he is either reinvesting them or using them to live on. Either way, it is a lot more comforting having the income.

Dividends paid by corporations result from their good performance, which results in cash accumulation. They send out this cash as reward to shareholders. Many companies have long-standing policies of raising dividends each year. There are dozens of companies that have raised their dividend every year for 30 years or more, which we refer to as dividend growers. There is a lot to love about dividend growers.

The chart below illustrates what happened to a person who was "unlucky" enough to have retired in 1999 with almost $3 million. He was unlucky due to retiring and investing right before the crash of the market, and dying right before the market turned around after the Great Recession in 2009. So he got none of the upside.

When he retired, he put the money in a dozen dividend-paying stocks. (I came up with these off the top of my head while driving back from a fishing trip. They were the first 12 stocks I thought of— no cherry picking!)

The Unluckiest Investor

Equity- 10,000 Shares	John Retires 1/1/1999	Market Low 10/9/2002	Market Low - John Dies 3/9/2009	Market Value 12/31/2014	Annual Return	Div/Share 1/1/1999	Div/Share 3/9/2009	Div/Share Increase
Coke	$ 233,700.00	$ 187,500.00	$ 164,300.00	$ 422,200.00	-3.41%	$ 0.32	$ 0.84	9.96%
Abbott Labs	$ 139,100.00	$ 122,100.00	$ 190,500.00	$ 447,800.00	3.14%	$ 0.28	$ 0.76	10.33%
General Mills	$ 129,300.00	$ 156,100.00	$ 209,600.00	$ 529,200.00	4.87%	$ 0.56	$ 0.88	4.55%
Walmart	$ 321,800.00	$ 409,900.00	$ 416,100.00	$ 858,800.00	2.56%	$ 0.25	$ 1.08	15.49%
Microsoft	$ 257,600.00	$ 159,600.00	$ 132,300.00	$ 464,500.00	-6.35%	$ -	$ 0.52	43.22%
Intel	$ 228,100.00	$ 101,000.00	$ 104,800.00	$ 362,900.00	-7.37%	$ 0.08	$ 0.56	21.11%
JNJ	$ 287,600.00	$ 407,700.00	$ 391,000.00	$ 1,045,700.00	3.07%	$ 0.52	$ 1.96	13.95%
PG	$ 309,300.00	$ 324,000.00	$ 374,100.00	$ 904,500.00	1.89%	$ 0.56	$ 1.66	11.29%
McDonalds	$ 275,200.00	$ 119,900.00	$ 442,400.00	$ 937,000.00	4.78%	$ 0.20	$ 2.00	25.44%
Chevron	$ 249,500.00	$ 231,100.00	$ 487,300.00	$ 1,121,800.00	6.81%	$ 1.32	$ 2.60	6.90%
Exxon	$ 256,300.00	$ 250,000.00	$ 564,900.00	$ 924,500.00	8.09%	$ 0.84	$ 1.68	7.06%
Home Depot	$ 299,400.00	$ 182,100.00	$ 156,600.00	$ 1,049,700.00	-6.18%	$ 0.08	$ 0.92	27.17%
Total	**$ 2,986,900.00**	**$ 2,651,000.00**	**$3,633,900.00**	**$ 9,068,600.00**	**1.94%**	**$ 5.01**	**$15.46**	**11.73%**

John's Income at Retirement:	$50,777.30	1.70%
John's Income at Death:	$161,292.60	5.40%

Annual Pay Raise of 11.73%

Read across the bottom of the chart. He starts out with $2,986,900. Three years later, his account is down to $2,651,000. When he dies six years later, his stock is worth $3,633,900, which is a return of only about 2% since he originally invested. Note that the stocks themselves are not worth much more than when he started. The *point,* however, is that even though his lump sum is not much greater after 11 years, his income has gone from $50,733.30 to $161,292.60. That is the power of rising dividends!

The implications for you when you buy and hold dividend-growing stocks is huge. The rate of increase on the dividends paid is one of the most reliable ways to stay ahead of inflation. Over the past 50 years, the rate of dividend increases has averaged 5.5%. In essence, that is a 5.5% pay increase for you each year. Let's take a look at how that looks with a famous example.

When Warren Buffett bought Coca-Cola (KO) in 1988, the dividend yield was around 4%. Today, the dividend yield is around 3%. How is that a good deal? It's a good deal because Coke has raised its dividend every year since he purchased it. When Buffett bought the stock for his company, Berkshire Hathaway (BRK), the dividend income he received on each $1 million invested was about $8,000. The split-adjusted price of the stock was $2.39. He has reinvested all of his dividends.

At the time of this writing, the stock is worth more than $40 per share and the amount of dividend income for every $1 million invested in 1988 is over $550,000. This $550,000 of income is what is called *yield on original investment*—which is around 55% for Buffett. The fact that Coke's share price has gone up twenty-fold is gravy. Incredibly, each million he invested is now worth $20 million and earning over $550,000 income. Warren is known to drink a Cherry Coke every day, and he can most certainly afford it. Plus, it contributes to his bottom line.

As you can see, Coke has been an outstanding long-term investment. Because of rising dividends, they have become an enormous source of income for countless investors, as well. This story can be told for hundreds of stocks. The ingredient to getting this type of investment is patience. There's no work. Make the purchase, then go play golf, go fishing, tinker in the yard, or read a book. No payroll to meet, no tenants to evict, etc.

In addition to making you a lot of money, dividends have psychological advantages as well. Dividends will help you weather any storm that comes your way, as long as you have the right perspective on them. One of the main reasons you are investing in dividend stocks is for income in the future. Let's look at an example of why you can rejoice when the market goes up or down when you own a dividend-grower.

Let's say you've bought stock in Great Dividend Grower, Inc. If share prices go up, you feel good about the investment. But what if they go down? I have learned that, with dividend-growers, I actually feel better when they go down in price. Why? Because my quarterly dividend will buy me more shares of the stock when it is down than when it is up. Remember, dividends are declared as an amount *per share*. So if your stock is paying $1 per share in dividends, it makes no difference what the price happens to be at the quarterly payment date; it will still pay out $1. The lower the share price, the more additional shares you get— and the bigger your dividend will be next quarter! You gotta love it.

What if the price just goes down and down? The truth is, it rarely will go too far in the real world with a great company—because the dividend gets so large that greed takes over and people buy the stock just for the dividend.

Example: Stock at $100 per share, with 2% yield
At $50.00, your yield goes to 4%
At $25.00, your yield goes to 8%
And if it fell all the way to $12.50, your yield would be 16%!

It is unlikely a good company would fall in price from $100 to $12.50. One of the things that would prevent it from doing so is that buyers would come in to get the high dividend.

If you own non-dividend-paying stocks, you have no advantage in the price going down. It just sits there until it goes up. If you have a $50 stock and it goes to $40, it will seem all negative—and it is. The only way to take advantage of the drop in value is to buy more shares. But buying more shares of a stock that is dropping is hard to do, so the dividend really takes the decision to buy more out of our hands, which is a good thing.

I don't mean that you should never own stocks that don't pay dividends. Some of the great companies out there should be owned at the right price, and, eventually, they may begin to pay dividends as well. Micron Technology (MU), the giant chipmaker that is the pride of my hometown of Boise, does not pay a dividend. But I own it because it is at a good value and I believe it may be a dividend-payer and grower in the future.

Some great companies have only recently begun to pay dividends. Starbucks (SBUX), Cisco (CSCO), Apple (AAPL), Gilead Sciences (GILD), Costco (COST), and Dunkin' Donuts (DNKN) are all companies that have started paying dividends within the last few years and have raised them rapidly. They are similar to Coca-Cola when Buffett bought his stake in 1988. To me, there is nothing more exciting than to hear that a company I own has increased its dividend payout. My future and current income is based on these dividend raises. Most workers would kill for a 5–10% pay raise per year. Over time, these increases can beat inflation and constitute real-world buying power.

I own many of these new payers, and I can tell you it is *fun*. There is really nothing fun about watching my Amazon (AMZN), Tesla (TSLA), and other no-dividend stock holdings bob up and down. Just isn't fun. It can be very profitable to own good growth stocks without dividends, but it's not *fun*. When the market is down, there is no psychological upside to it in any way. So make dividend growers a big part of your portfolio and it may be a lot better time for you in the next big downturn.

A quick caveat: It is very important that you don't chase high yields. Many times a high yield is not a good sign, or it is a company such as a utility, which has steady high dividends but little growth. You also need to be sure to have a lot of good companies, because, sooner or later, one of them will have to cut or lower their dividend. It is not particularly difficult to avoid this problem. The cash hordes of good companies keep paying off recession after recession.

It is conceivable that a person with $2 million dollars at retirement who is taking $60,000 a year in income could grow that income to $250,000 in 20 years of dividend increases.

The $2 million may be some higher amount, but as we have seen it is "what the pile can buy" that counts. We see a lot of wealthy 60-year-olds who think they can retire and enjoy a good lifestyle by taking interest from bonds. If they own 20-year bonds, their income is no higher in 20 years than the day they retired. So if you intend to live on bonds, CDs, or annuities for an extended period, you had better start with a very large amount.

Chapter 11 Takeaways:

1. Dividend-paying stocks as a group have outperformed non-dividend stocks.

2. The rate of growth of dividends is one of the few ways to stay ahead of inflation.

3. Good companies who have recently started dividend payments usually grow their payouts at a rate higher than old, established dividend payers.

4. Owning dividend stocks increases your comfort level when stocks go down.

Mindful Money Questions:

1. What does yield on original investment mean and how is it calculated?

2. Why do dividend-paying stocks usually do better in down markets?

3. Why can you feel good about a decrease in the share price of a dividend-paying stock?

CHAPTER 12

What Should Your Portfolio Consist Of?

Now let's take a look at what our client's portfolio will look like. Investors need two main things: They need growth and they need a portfolio that encourages them to stick with that growth. The boost of courage can come from us, but mostly it comes from knowing that your holdings are likely to buy more and more shares if the market drops, by the reinvestment of dividends. If you own all growth stocks, it is very tough to hang in from peak to trough and back to peak. It can take years and years.

What is actually in your portfolio depends mostly on your time frame that you have to invest. If you are 40, your portfolio will look much different than if you are 65 and need income. In general, we add more and more income as a client approaches retirement. Our average retired client earns a yield of around 5.75%. We accomplish that by adding income-intensive investments to the mix, and by holding on to the dividend-growing stocks and let them increase the income. There are generally two kinds of investors: One is the accumulator and the other is in the income phase. These usually overlap, at least for a while, as clients enter retirement.

Our firm's philosophy is that the path to get there is to own predominately companies that grow earnings and dividends each year and have a good probability of doing that. That sounds pretty simple—and it is. So why not just do that and forget it? Because as you know by now, as Tom Petty so memorably put it, "the waiting is the hardest part." (See figure 4.)

These charts are typical of what you will find online, and it's worth doing some additional research on your own. I say this because if an

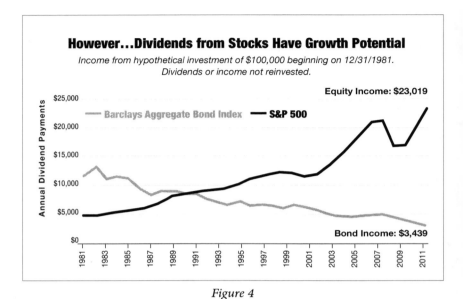

Figure 4

asset class is overwhelmingly known as having better returns with less risk and less volatility, it would make sense that everyone would be on to that. But they are not on to it. Because, as Buffett once said, "Ships will sail around the world and the Flat Earth Society will flourish." The Flat Earth Society in this case is advisors and financial media, who will try to convince you that you need to be "doing something."

In addition to dividend increasers, we believe that certain regions and certain industries will outperform at times or even for a very long time. Health care and energy are good examples of this, and may earn an overweight position.

Mutual Funds and Exchange Traded Funds (ETFs)
When we get into smaller companies or foreign stocks, our tendency is to use fund managers that we like in those areas rather than trying to select individual companies. We use ETFs in some cases.

Closed-End Funds
These can occasionally be bought at large discounts to the underlying stocks, because they trade on the basis of supply and demand. Unlike

regular (open-end funds), which trade at the actual value of the underlying stocks at the close of the market each day. Closed-end funds distribute a set amount each year that is managed. The payout is usually a combination of dividends and projected capital gains. By doing this, you can take income without selling shares—or you can average back in on regular intervals if you are an accumulator.

Master Limited Partnerships

Our firm uses master limited partnerships (MLPs) in many portfolios for their tax advantages and high income. They are complex enough that I won't get into more detail here; I recommend doing separate research on your own to learn more about them.

Real Estate Investment Trusts (REITs)

We think it is important to have access to real estate markets, but you don't have to be a landlord! REITs make it easy to invest, because you're letting experts buy, sell, and manage the properties (and you don't get any middle-of-the-night complaints about broken air conditioners or burst pipes). Yields and growth can be a good combination for 10–20% of your portfolio.

Growth Stocks

Dividend-payers are the foundation of our approach, but you can't ignore overwhelming growth stories like Apple or Amazon, among many others. We look to buy these when they are at attractive values, and they tend to go low when people panic. Be patient, and eventually investors will panic and you will get some of these great companies for a bargain. As mentioned above, great growth stocks sometimes become great dividend stocks as they mature. In many cases, companies who pay their first dividend will tend to raise dividends a lot in the first 10 or 20 years.

Bonds

Bonds have already been covered, but, in general, we avoid them. At the time this book was published, the U.S. was in its 32nd year of falling interest rates—which has created a 32-year bull market for bonds. As you recall, the only way to have your bonds go up in price is to have rates go down, and, for now, there is not much room to go down. The interest on bonds is extremely low, and, even when they are attractive, they will not increase your income over time. (I usually don't like bonds—can you tell?) The huge exception to this is for clients who have a lot of money and are older. If you are 85 and are already very wealthy, don't want any drama, and just want to preserve your money for the next generation, then bonds are a fine place to store a certain portion of your money. They may keep you wealthy, they just won't get you wealthy.

Unregistered Products

There are a few one-offs that come up, such as private real estate or stock offerings. We don't deal with a lot of that. There are people who will want you to get into start-up companies on the ground floor or initial public offerings. I think that is OK for a small amount of money. The track record of start-ups is not good, and if the stock is offered without being registered (known as a *Regulation D* or "Reg D" offering) it may be a great deal, but it is very, very rare. The same goes for penny stocks. They are cheap for a reason. The decision is yours, but I would stay away from those, too.

As a general rule, I would never buy an unregistered security. What is the difference? Reg D securities are offered without being registered with the SEC. The sales presentation can claim all kinds of projections. They are not audited. They may have zero cash. If you and I had an idea, we could offer a Reg D stock in a short time to raise money for a company. We just go out, rent a room, and start talking. The only way that a person should invest is to know the project and business plan personally and to understand it thoroughly. You must be an accredited investor ($1.5 million of investable assets) to get into these. But there is usually no way to verify that status. Some people will just sign the form, say they have the money, and they are owners. Good luck writing it off on your taxes when it goes away. But the pitch is so good, sometimes using celebrities or politicians as speakers, that this stuff gets bought. Again if you don't know that it has a solid premise and exceptional management, run fast. Better yet, don't go to the sales pitch at all.

Securities Investor Protection Corporation (SIPC) Insurance

Always make sure you deal with someone who is covered by the SIPC. Dealers that are covered have to display the sign in a conspicuous place in the office. If you are not sure, ask.

Here's how the organization describes itself: "SIPC protects against the loss of cash and securities—such as stocks and bonds—held by a customer at a SIPC-member brokerage firm. The limit of SIPC protection is $500,000, which includes a $250,000 limit for cash. Most customers of failed brokerage firms when assets are missing from customer accounts are protected. There is no requirement that a customer reside in or be a citizen of the United States. A non-U.S. citizen with an account at a brokerage firm that is a member of SIPC is treated the same as a resident or citizen of the United States with an account at a brokerage firm that is a member of SIPC."

Annuities

Annuities get a bad rap, but they are not evil. They are not for everyone, and some are better than others. I can't get on the internet, it seems, without a picture of *Forbes* writer and money manager Ken Fisher with a quote below him that says, "I hate annuities and so should you!" Fisher can't sell annuities because his reps don't have insurance licenses. They are an insurance product.

People usually hate what they can't sell. Ford dealers hate Chevys. Chevy dealers hate Fords. Money managers who charge fees and only work with cookie-cutter portfolios hate annuities.

Since annuities are an insurance product, what do they insure? They insure that you will not outlive a guaranteed amount of predetermined income in the future. The most popular types of annuities give you returns based on stock market indexes or funds. These will go up with up markets, and in years when the market is down, they give you a guaranteed rate of return. Currently that is around 2%—even if the market goes down 20%, your account still grows by 2%. The upside is capped to around currently 7% in up years. Not too good. When you find caps over 10%, it makes them more attractive. These are called *equity index annuities.*

Variable annuities with income base guarantees allow you to take the better of the underlying subaccounts (which are run like mutual funds) or a guaranteed rate, perhaps 5–6%. You invest for 10 years, and get your choice of the market return or the guarantee. The guarantee then pays out income based on that amount. It is not available as a lump sum.

If a client is building a retirement account and wants a portion of maybe 10–20% that is absolutely guaranteed, it can be a good fit. We can calculate an amount of exact income based on the guarantee. Sometimes we will put enough in an annuity to double Social Security benefits, for example. As you know by now, I believe the market will outperform these types of investments over the long run. But there is something very reassuring about having another stream of guaranteed income for life along with Social Security or pensions.

No one can offer the guarantees that life insurance companies can. They are not regulated by the government and they have a very high standard of self-regulation. They are required to keep an overwhelming amount of reserves to make good on their promises. To me, the life insurance companies are like cockroaches: They are the only survivors in a nuclear economic scenario. Mind you, I don't believe in a nuclear economic scenario, but many people do. So, if they want a small part guaranteed, we don't blame them. Don't let anyone shame you out of owning an annuity.

To my knowledge there has never been a life insurance company that reneged on an annuity payout or death benefit. Don't get me wrong. Absolutely horrible life insurance policies and annuities get sold all the time. But receiving your payout is one worry you shouldn't have. Just be sure to know the rules going in, because they can be confusing and have a lot of rules.

The problem comes with the companies offering horrible products that pay out huge commissions and the agents that want to sell them. You need to be careful. But there are also some fine products, especially when interest rates are higher. In the current interest rate environment, we rarely write annuity contracts, due to low rates and guarantees. When rates were high and guarantees were 6–7%, they were very attractive. That's when I bought mine.

Sooner or later, the annuity haters talk someone out of a lifetime of guarantees, the market goes way down, and someone gets sued.

Annuities serve a place in retirement planning. In fact, the government has been talking lately about using annuities to fund accounts that will help end Social Security. And in reality, annuities are the only instrument they could use to do this while guaranteeing a Social Security-like stream of guaranteed payments.

Chapter 12 Takeaways:

1. Do your homework on the various investment types if you are not familiar with them.

2. Get up to speed on rising dividend stocks and why you should own them.

3. Consider owning good growth stocks, too, and possibly REITs and MLPs.

4. Diversify wisely with smart fund managers in areas you don't feel confident in.

SECTION THREE
MINDFULNESS: TO BE AWARE
IS ALL WE CAN DO

"My life has been full of terrible misfortunes,
most of which never happened."

—Michel de Montaigne

When I use the word *mindfulness,* I mean it in the sense of knowing what is going on in your own head. In an ideal world, you'd be able to access that information at any time—although it might drive you crazy. Even so, when you take the time to practice, it can be a very good habit.

In this section, I will describe long-term improvements you can make to put yourself on the road to wealth. As part of that, I'll discuss new studies about the human brain and how it can be changed. More important, I will lay out a proven formula to alter the habits that keep you from being successful with your finances. This step is the key to change the number-one variable in your success: *your own behavior.* It doesn't involve psychobabble or New Age hocus-pocus. It's proven research, some of which has been around for more than six decades, and it has been proven to work in real life. The ideas presented about changing habits and thought patterns are fast and effective.

In the preceding pages, I have made the case that it is not the market that destroys your dreams and goals—it's your brain, making poor decisions, panicking, and getting consumed in the fear-and-greed cycle. Do you have to even be in the cycle? No! You can choose to ignore it.

Because that ability doesn't come naturally to most of us, we must learn the skills to protect our hard-earned assets. As with any worthy pursuit, it will take willpower to develop the correct habits—but rest assured, they will help you in all areas of life in which you sabotage your wants and needs.

The key to avoiding investment errors is to grow your ability to simply ignore the market. A 10-year trip to the moon—in which you don't see or hear of the stock market and you reinvest dividends—is a sure winner.

If you want a dark perspective on our ability to change, hey, just ask a German philosopher:

"Everyone believes himself, a priori, perfectly free—even in his individual actions, and thinks that at every moment he can commence another manner of life.... But a posteriori, through experience, he finds to his astonishment that he is not free, but subjected to necessity, that in spite of all his resolutions and reflections he does not change his conduct, and that from the beginning of his life to the end of it, he must carry out the very character which he himself condemns..." —On the Freedom of the Will, Schopenhauer

That philosophy won't get you very far in investing. Yes, changing habits and thought patterns can be difficult. Just as medicine has kept us from dying of infections and diseases, however, the science of the brain is revealing new ways to make changes that last.

What is it about us that makes us not only believe wrong things but makes us believe them even after we see evidence to the contrary? More than 50 years ago, University of Minnesota social psychologist Leon Festinger provided his perspective in *When Prophecy Fails*:

"A man with a conviction is a hard man to change. Tell him you disagree and he turns away. Show him facts or figures and he questions your sources. Appeal to logic and he fails to see your point.

"We have all experienced the futility of trying to change a strong conviction, especially if the convinced person has some investment in his belief. We are familiar with the variety of ingenious defenses with which people protect their convictions, managing to keep them unscathed through the most devastating attacks.

"But man's resourcefulness goes beyond simply protecting a belief. Suppose an individual believes something with his whole heart; suppose further that he has a commitment to this belief, that he has taken irrevocable actions because of it; finally, suppose that he is presented with evidence, unequivocal and undeniable evidence, that his belief is wrong: what will happen? The individual will frequently emerge, not only unshaken, but even more convinced of the truth of his beliefs than ever before. Indeed, he may even show a new fervor about convincing and converting other people to his view."

As you go through the remainder of the book, I recommend that you start a list titled "50 things I know that may not be true." Write them down as a statement, not a question. For instance, instead of asking "Is the president the Antichrist?" write "The president may not be the Antichrist."

Be honest with yourself. Many things you accept as true will be beliefs and not facts. If it is a belief, you must admit there is at least some chance that it is not true. It may be hard to come up with 50, but once you get the hang of it you will keep thinking of things. Your list may look like this:

1. The President may not be the Antichrist.
2. Pointers may be better bird dogs than retrievers.
3. I can't learn a foreign language.
4. I am ahead in poker games year to date.
5. I'll never be able to stop slicing my drives.

You get the idea. This section is not meant to give your brain a complete reboot, but I believe it is a good start. If you're interested in diving deeper on the subject, I highly recommend *Feeling Good* by Dr. David Burns and *You Are Not Your Brain* by Dr. Jeffrey Schwartz.

CHAPTER 13

You Are Not Your Brain

"A man is what he thinks about all day long."

—Emerson

Your body is an incredible mechanism, and the least understood organ within it is the brain. There's no simple answer to "Where do thoughts come from?" Science largely believes thoughts are just the firing of neurons in the brain, a concept that works well for our purposes—and we'll leave aside religious beliefs and competing scientific theories for simplicity's sake.

Just as the heart pumps blood and the kidneys filter blood, your brain produces thoughts. Once the thoughts are produced, someone has to think about them. That is where consciousness comes in. Even with all the technology at our disposal, how or why we are conscious remains a mystery. Again, in the interest of simplicity, let's consider the two main theories. The first says that consciousness originates in the atoms that compose brain tissue, through organic processes and brain matter. This theory says that our consciousness is like everyone else's, but we see it as a unique perspective. If true, we are nothing more than automatons reacting to the laws of physics and chemistry. Free will is not usually assumed in this school of thought. Of course, that would have tremendous implications about choice and freedom, the judicial system, etc.

The other theory depends on an entity such as the mind, spirit, or soul as the seat of consciousness. This entity observes our thoughts and is conscious. How it happens no one knows, and that's OK for an investment book. I am not a philosopher, and certainly not a brooding German one who believes human desire is futile.

The philosophy that the mind is separate from the brain, known as dualism, has been debated for centuries. It is what Descartes had in mind when he said, "I think, therefore I am." (The idea that the brain alone, atoms and molecules, can by itself give rise to the depths of all human consciousness is a relatively new idea.)

As the brain produces and introduces thoughts to your consciousness, you can ignore them or focus on them. The mind makes moral and qualitative judgments about the thought. Let's say a man (who wants to be faithful) has a sexual thought about someone who is not his spouse. He now will most likely make a moral and qualitative judgment about the thought that he had no control over. For instance, he may think the sexual thought is *wrong* and that the person he is thinking about is *attractive*. Those are thoughts of the will. They are not automatic.

The question of free will is debated all the time. We have no control over the thoughts that are fired at us, but you do get to choose if you focus on the thought or reject the thought. This has been referred to as *free won't*. While we may be helpless in preventing the thought, we do apparently control the focus. And it is the focus that makes actual changes in the brain.

The point, for our purposes, is that you have to know that what I have described as the *mind* can make real changes, actual physical changes, in the brain. This ability for the brain to change, even as we age, is relatively new science. This concept of the brain creating new physical matter (neurons) by the willful focus of the mind was confirmed in the late 1990s. This new science is called *neuroplasticity*. Neuroscientific research indicates that experience can actually change both the brain's physical structure (i.e., anatomy) and functional organization.

During most of the 20th century, scientists believed that anatomical changes were only possible in the brains of infants and the very young. But, using advanced brain imaging and scanning, neuro changes could be observed in adult subjects who underwent a regimen of several weeks of training their thoughts.

How unbelievable is that? Well, it was interesting enough for me to obsess about it for weeks and reading all I could find on it. If it were true, and it is, it could be the most important breakthrough we have seen in a long time. If humans could willfully change the operation of their brains, the possibilities would be endless. I came across the books and research of Dr. Jeffrey Schwartz. His book *The Mind and the Brain* details his research in the '80s and '90s with Dr. Albert Stapp.

This requires agreement on some basic ideas. We must reject the idea that humans have no control over their thoughts and actions. This seems easy, but science has been rejecting the role of free will for some time. Dr. Schwartz has spent much of his life proving that human will or *volition* plays a central role in how our brains are conditioned to think. I am not asking you to reject science. The fact is we will probably never understand consciousness completely. I am just asking you to act on what you probably already believe to be true: that you have some control over what thoughts you focus on and your actions.

Let's talk about two concepts that are important if we are to become successful investors. The first one is the concept of our "true selves."

Dr. Schwartz describes it as follows: "Living according to your true self means seeing yourself for who you really are based on your sincere striving to embody the values and achieve the goals you truly believe in."

The concept of your true self is important. This concept implies that, within each of us, there are two: *the person we are and the person we aspire to be.* You can think of the true self as "who we aspire to be." Because we are human, we will never completely be our true selves. (Some people believe we can attain that state, known in spiritual circles as *self-actualization*.)

Second, Dr. Schwartz defines a defective thought as *any false or inaccurate thought or any unhelpful or distracting impulse, urge, or desire that takes you away from your true goals and true self.*

Once you realize your true self (your baseline values), you can easily recognize defective brain messages.

Much of Dr. Schwartz's research was done in the field of obsessive compulsive disorder (OCD). OCD provides a unique view into free will. OCD patients suffer from constant unwanted thoughts—for instance, the need to wash one's hands constantly. What is interesting here is that the patients often realize that the thoughts and impulses are false. Until the thoughts are recognized as false, no healing of the disorder can begin.

> *A defective thought is defined as: Any false or inaccurate thought or any unhelpful or distracting impulse, urge, or desire that takes you away from your true goals and true self.*

Dr. Schwartz developed a therapy which involves viewing our thoughts as a third-party observer. This therapy acknowledges that we are not responsible for thoughts or impulses that bombard us, but *are* responsible to our reactions to those initial thoughts. He developed the *Four Steps* as a therapy to change how we are effected by false brain messages. Here is an overview of the Four Steps.

1. Relabel. This initial step acknowledges that our thought is wrong. Let's say you get the thought "I need to move my money out of the market before the election." You can recognize that thought as false, since it involves knowing the future—which is always a sign that a thought is false and is in fact a deceptive brain message. By giving it a new label, you take away its power.

2. Reframe. So, now you must give that thought a framework, which says what it *really* is. For instance, you may say, "That is not me, it's just my anxiety, it's just my brain!" You acknowledge it has no basis in reality.

3. Refocus: Here is where you recognize control and free will. You refocus your attention on an activity or mental process that is wholesome, productive, and in line with your true self. This is where your "veto" option comes in, and you exercise "free won't."

4. Revalue: Now it's time to go back and dismiss the deceptive thoughts for what they are. They have no purpose and no value in moving you toward your goals.

Although it couldn't be demonstrated scientifically until recent years, the concept has some history to it. As the Apostle Paul said in *Romans 7:18:* "For I have the desire to do what is good, but I cannot carry it out." Paul wanted to do the right thing, but found himself unable to and ended up calling himself a wretched man. Later in the book, however, he says, "Do not be conformed to the world but be transformed by the renewing of your mind." There it is! Two thousand years ago, long before the invention of MRI and PET scans, the cure for man was to use his mind to change the mind—and therefore the brain.

Failing to carry out what we want to do is obviously not a new problem. To be a good investor, you must execute. In many cases, that means doing what we don't feel like doing, but what we know is right.

There are three major qualities that I have observed in successful investors, and I don't mean making three fortunes and losing three fortunes. I am talking about sustaining and growing long-term wealth. Quick riches and losses are for entrepreneurs, inventors, and professional entertainers and athletes. Even if you believe you can make it all in one shot, you still need these qualities to hang onto it. When you have money, everyone else wants it—and can concoct countless reasons to get you to give it to them.

So, what are these three qualities?

1. The ability to postpone gratification in all areas of life. Take what you have earned and are ready for, not what you think you have to have now.

2. A realistic worldview. This is just a willingness to look at what has happened or is happening, and to act on those facts. You must have an open and flexible way of thinking.

3. The 100% acceptance of responsibility. You control your decisions and can't blame anyone else for the ones you make.

No one exhibits all three all the time, and there are other minor traits that can be helpful. But, when you boil it all down, they are the qualities that I know I need to have and need to work toward with as much energy as possible.

I have been in the investment business, and studying investment psychology, for almost 30 years. I have always wondered why people behave in ways that are counterproductive to their own purposes and true selves. Why do we desire to act one way, yet continue to act in ways that are not in our best interest? To me that became a fascinating question about myself and about my clients.

The problem is that we don't react to the facts, but rather to *defective thoughts* that are automatically produced by our brains.

As discussed previously, we don't control these thoughts, but we can control our reactions to them. This has been the foundation for cognitive therapy since the late 1950s.

No amount of investment knowledge and techniques can replace the three qualities of successful investors cited above. This book places the responsibility for financial success directly on the only entity who can control outcomes: ourselves. We must face ourselves. We must look within to do battle, and not wish all the "bad people" would go away. We can't change them.

Being able to change ourselves and change the way we react to life's events is a much bigger factor than any change we may exert on the world. People like Gandhi, Buddha, and Mother Teresa may have changed the world, but none of them cared about investments. The most profound thing we can do for ourselves, our families, and the world is to change *ourselves*.

A lot of nonsense is found in the investment world, generated by those who sell newsletters and magazines as well as by genuine criminals. But neither the sensational financial media nor the crooks are to blame. While there is no good reason to do business with criminals or listen to news that promotes fear and greed, we seem to think more clearly about buying fresh vegetables than when it comes to our hard-earned savings and investments.

Let's consider an example. You may not realize it, but Bernie Madoff never sold registered securities. He was never audited by an outside authority, nor was he required to do reporting under SEC guidelines. It's the same problem with legitimate hedge funds: a total lack of transparency. Madoff called his strategy a *black box* that used a *secret formula*. Amazingly, he never provided a narrative to his clients of how he invested. Madoff was one case where you wanted to be more than six degrees from Kevin Bacon. Bacon lost a small fortune with Madoff, as did Steven Spielberg, Sandy Koufax, Larry King, and many more.

People who gave him their money—and many of them were famous and successful—made their investments out of greed. People invest because of what they *think*, and it's easy to believe things they know deep, deep down aren't right. Humans are greatly motivated by fear and greed. I have invested in scams, and you may have done the same. It's because we made decisions not on what we knew, but on what we wanted to believe.

We seem to be more focused when picking fresh vegetables than when it comes to our hard-earned savings and investments.

No one can scam us without our permission. The cons need us to participate. After the fact, we're left saying "I knew that guy was crooked" or "I knew that sounded too good to be true." We have to believe in things that are wrong and *we* make the choice. Is that a little harsh? Yes, it is but the truth is harsh in many cases. Investment scams will always exist as long as we stay willing customers. Pamela Meyer, author of *Lie Spotting*, says, "A lie has no power whatsoever by its mere utterance, its power emerges when someone else agrees to believe it…lying is a cooperative act."

The mind, like the true self, is simply *you*. It was you when you were a newborn, a know-it-all teenager, and on your 80th birthday. Personality changes, your body changes, you may have even changed political parties, but all the while there is something that is just *you*.

For this book to be effective, you need to know what goes wrong in your brain when you make expensive mistakes with your investments. It is also important to know when you are likely responding to nonsense, i.e., defective brain messages. With this knowledge, you can step back and assess your thinking as a third-party observer.

This observance of thoughts as they happen—a.k.a., mindfulness—is a habit that only comes with lots of practice and meditation. You can start out by simply counting your thoughts as they come. Some people find it helpful to think of this "third-party observer" as someone who is advocating for you. This wise advocate is always aware of your best interests and knows your true self. In spiritual terms, for instance, a Christian may view this knowledge as guidance by the Holy Spirit.

No matter how you arrive at your wise advocate, the main point is to realize that you are not held hostage to random thoughts thrown off from your brain. You do not have to go into an adrenaline-fueled fit every time you hear something on CNBC, whether it's appealing to your fear or greed, or a little of both.

CHAPTER 14

The Ten Basic Thinking Errors

*"Studies have shown that 90% of error in thinking
is due to error in perception. If you can change your perception,
you can change your emotion and this can lead to new ideas."*

—Edward de Bono, author of *Six Thinking Hats*

The idea that most humans suffer from basic thinking errors (a.k.a., *cognitive errors*) has been around for more than 60 years. Dr. Aaron T. Beck taught and researched at the University of Pennsylvania and is considered the father of cognitive therapy. *Cognitive therapy*, as opposed to Freudian-style psychoanalysis, asserts that mental discomfort is not necessarily caused by past trauma or life events. It says that depression, anxiety, rumination, guilt, and many other negative feelings can be attributed to the thoughts we are thinking *right now*.

One of the classic thinking errors, for example, is referred to as *mind reading*. We can all relate. We pass an acquaintance on the street, believe we make eye contact, but the person doesn't acknowledge us—leading to the feeling of being snubbed. "I must not be important to him," you may tell yourself. Now, think about the same situation with the knowledge that the acquaintance's daughter had been injured at a softball game. He's rushing, preoccupied, and might not stop if he ran into his favorite Hollywood star. The discomfort felt is from the *thoughts we tell ourselves*—based on our own thinking error, not an actual negative event. Removing distorted thoughts alleviates mental discomfort.

Of course, the key to investment success is thinking the right thoughts and not having fear, greed, anxiety, etc., rule our investment decisions. When it comes to the news or financial media, or talking about investments at a party, we are not affected by the actual events, but by the meaning we assign them in our heads.

If Beck was the father of cognitive therapy, Dr. David Burns is his heir. His book, *Feeling Good, The New Mood Therapy*, has sold more than 5 million copies and continues to sell to new readers. Dr. Burns' list of 10 cognitive thinking errors has been tweaked over time by different authors, and different terms are used at times, but there is agreement on the basic list. Six of the errors are highly relevant to the investment world; I've summarized all ten below:

1. **All-or-Nothing Thinking**: You see things in black-and-white categories. If your performance falls short of perfect, you see yourself as a total failure. The advantage of this is that it is more predictable and creates the feeling there is order in the world around you. This, in turn, should give you an edge to controlling your world. Unfortunately, it doesn't work that way. Uncertainty is all we have. Living comfortably with uncertainty is possible, but it takes time to master. The skills you are about to learn will help.

2. **Overgeneralization**: You see a single negative event as a never-ending pattern of defeat. If you wake up in more pain you may think, "I'll never be able to enjoy anything, anymore." Misery does love company, but globalizing misfortune in this way creates an exaggerated sense of rejection and loneliness.

3. **Mental Filter**: You pick out a single negative detail and dwell on it exclusively, so that your vision of all reality becomes darkened, like the drop of ink that discolors the entire beaker of water. For example, you are preparing lunch for some friends and discover that you do not have an essential ingredient to make a dish that you were planning to include. All you can think about is how the whole lunch will be ruined. It gives you indigestion.

4. **Disqualifying the Positive or "D the P"**: You reject positive experiences by insisting they "don't count" for some reason. In this way, you can maintain a negative belief that is contradicted by your

everyday experiences. For instance, a friend comes over and tells you that you look great. Your immediate thought is: "I don't feel great. She doesn't understand." Maybe not, but try a simple "thank you."

5. **Jumping to Conclusions:** You make a negative interpretation even though there are no definite facts that convincingly support you conclusions.

   A. **Mind Reading**: You arbitrarily conclude that someone is reacting negatively to you, and you don't bother to check this out. For example, you pass a coworker in the hallway and say "Hi" and he doesn't respond. You think, *He must be upset with me, what did I do wrong?* When you check it out, you find that the coworker was preoccupied about a sick child he had just left at home.

   B. **The Fortune-Teller Error**: You anticipate that things will turn out badly, and you feel convinced that your prediction is an established fact. For example, you wake up with a headache and think "Now my whole day is ruined. I had so much to do and I'll never get it all done."

6. **Catastrophizing or Minimization**: You exaggerate the importance of things, or you inappropriately shrink things until they appear tiny (your own desirable qualities or the other fellow's imperfections). If you find yourself experiencing a flare-up of lower back pain and find yourself saying "I can't stand this, I can't take this anymore!" As a matter of fact, however, you can, though you may not want to. In minimization, however, you take positive qualities or events and deny them their importance. For instance, someone comments on how nice it is to see you at an outing and you say, "Lot of good it does if I can't participate in the activities."

7. **Emotional Reasoning**: You assume that your negative emotions necessarily reflect the way things really are: "I feel it, therefore it must be true." For example you think "I feel useless, therefore I am useless."

8. **Labeling and Mislabeling:** This is an extreme form of overgeneralization. Instead of describing your error, you attach a negative label to yourself: "I'm a loser." When someone else's

behavior rubs you the wrong way, you attach a negative label to them. "He's a xyz louse." Instead of seeing yourself as an individual who has a pain problem, you find yourself saying, "I'm defective, broken, and without any redeemable qualities."

9. **Personalization:** You see yourself as the cause of some negative external event, which, in fact, you were not primarily responsible for. For example, you and your spouse go out to eat at a fancy restaurant, but the food and the service are poor. You find yourself feeling responsible for making a bad choice and "ruining" your evening together.

10. **Should Statements**: You try to motivate yourself with *should* and *shouldn't*, as if you had to be whipped and punished before you could be expected to do anything. *Must* and *ought* are also offenders. The emotional consequence is guilt, and these statements set you up for feeling resentful and pressured. They also imply that you are complying with an external authority. When you direct should statements toward others you feel anger, frustration, and resentment.

How Do They Apply to Investing?

Overgeneralization. You see a single event as a never-ending pattern of defeat. This is also known as the *extrapolation error*. Many investors are constantly extrapolating far into the future from what happened yesterday or today. For instance, the market is crashing and your mind starts to wander about losing all of your retirement savings. Or the market is going up sharply and you think of the how much money you will have if it goes up to a certain point.

Disqualifying the positive. Because of the way our brains work, the fear of loss is greater than the promise of gain—and we may fail to have positive feelings from actual positive events. For instance, the market is up 20% in the middle of the year, but falls in October to the point it's up only 10%. Your focus may now be on the fact that you are down from midyear. You may completely disqualify the good news that you are still up 10%. The "highest amount it ever was" is a silly barometer of success.

Another example can be seen in dividend-paying stocks that you plan to hold for 20 years: If you don't see the beauty of dividends reinvesting in cheaper shares when prices dip (and in turn creating potentially higher dividends), you're disqualifying the positive.

Fortune-teller error. I consider this the mother of all investment thinking errors. You're not omnipotent and you don't know the future. When you invest and you happen to be right, that sets up a delusion that your prediction was right—when it only means the company did well or the market in general went up after you bought and raised your stock with it. It also involves all manner of trying to predict geopolitical cycles, short-term market moves, and trying to extrapolate outcomes by listening to the news financial media. Watch out, because this one can cause serious grief and big losses.

Emotional reasoning. This error makes you think what you feel is *reality*, when actually it is only what you feel. I can't tell you how many times I have been on the phone with a client who said, "I feel like the market is going to crash." In fact, if I get enough of these calls, I have a decent case for market bottom, not a top! Almost every piece of financial media commentary is based on emotional reasoning.

Labeling and mislabeling. This error will make you say things like "this stock is a piece of s***," "I was an idiot for not getting out of that stock," or "I'm an idiot." A better way of framing it is to say "I acted foolishly in this case." As much as you tell yourself you are an idiot, it is not only false, it is counterproductive to making money in stocks. This does you no good and, in fact, labeling things may make you fall into other thinking errors that will cost you money.

Should statements. *Should statements*, like the fortune-telling error, trap you into the idea that you are all-knowing (omnipotence error). In investing, the big two are:

1. "I knew I should have bought that stock!"
2. "I knew I should have sold that stock!"

Note that these statements also have the fortune-telling error in them, so it's a double beat-down to your psyche.

You may really feel, with 20/20 hindsight, like you should have known or seen something that would have prevented a poor decision. If you did a poor job researching the stock or bought it on a whim it won't matter—because that is another behavioral problem, which is lack of faith. You are better off thinking accurate thoughts that move you to your goal, such as: "In the future I will not buy a stock unless I have available all the information I need. When I make a decision that is all I can do. Some will go up and some won't, but I'm not omniscient."

Now what?

If you can avoid these thinking errors, you can be a lot happier. The first step, therefore, is to memorize them. Keep a file card in your pocket with all of them written down, and review them for 15 minutes a day for two or three weeks. If you revert to your past thinking behaviors, make sure to do a regular tune-up.

CHAPTER 15

Tricks Our Minds Play On Us

"Permanent loss in a well-diversified equity portfolio is always a human achievement, of which the market itself is incapable."

—Nick Murray

The errors listed in the previous chapter aren't the only ones *Homo sapiens* repeat over and over. Despite our big brains, we are easily fooled by illusions of thinking as we are by optical illusions. The following are the logical fallacies and biases that inflict the most damage on the decisions and behavior of advisors and their clients.

The Anchoring Effect

At a conference for investment advisors I attended a few years ago, the keynote speaker walked out on stage, and with no introduction, he declared loudly, "I can tell each one of you the *exact* amount that each of your clients has in their accounts." This outlandish statement grabbed our collective attention, as you might guess. Following a long pause, he delivered these astounding words of wisdom: "*The highest amount it ever was.*"

Yes, indeed, he had hit the number exactly.

As investors, we fixate on the price of a stock or the value of our portfolio at its highest point or where we bought in. If we buy a stock at $100 and it goes to $50, it can become our life's goal to only sell when the stock gets back to $100. This psychological effect is called *anchoring*, and it can be very costly. The better approach is to look at each stock as if you just got it, and then evaluate the prospects at the current price. Anything else forces you to keep (which is the same as buying) a horrible investment just because you have a number anchored in your head.

I vividly remember a client who had $1.5 million in his account at the peak. By the time he came to us, it had fallen to about $1.2 million. He said he was "tired of losing money"—even though he hadn't. About two years later, his account value had been boosted to $1.35 million. He left us, however, complaining that we hadn't made him money either. Despite the growth in his account, he was convinced that he was still losing money, because he was anchored on the highest amount his account ever touched.

In *Thinking Fast and Slow,* psychologist Daniel Kahneman talks about two brain systems that we use to determine our entire world. System One is the system that ballparks everything, looking at past events quickly to put a value on things happening now. Rules of thumb, collected over a lifetime, are called *heuristics,* which account for the majority of how we come to conclusions (or worse, *jump to conclusions,* one of Dr. Burns' 10 basic errors). Kahneman's System Two is our more deliberate self. It is contemplative by nature and demands correct figures and logic. It is underused in the investment world. Anchoring can have peculiar effects on our decisions. The mere suggestion of a number can make us anchor to that number, such as the asking price for a house. We give more value to the higher-priced one in two similar situations.

Kahneman describes performing an experiment with a roulette wheel that was numbered from 0–100, but rigged to stop on only two numbers, 10 and 65. Researchers would spin the wheel and ask the subjects to write down the number, which of course was 10 or 65, and then posed two questions:

1. Is the percentage of African nations in the U.N. larger or smaller than you wrote?

2. What is your best guess for the number of African nations in the U.N.?

A roulette wheel cannot possibly yield useful information about the percentage of African nations in the U.N. The participants should have simply ignored the numbers, but they didn't! The average estimate of the students whose wheel stopped at 10 was 25%, while it was 45% for those who saw 65. The anchoring effect caused people to place value in a number totally unrelated to the facts. Try it yourself: Ask someone if Gandhi died at 114 years old, and you will get a much higher estimate of his age at death than if you ask if he died at 45.

The Extrapolation Error

Extrapolation is an act or instance of inferring an unknown from something that is known. For instance, we are 60 miles from a huge cliff, speeding across the desert at 60 miles per hour. Extrapolate that, and we will fall over the cliff and die in 60 minutes. Sure, that could be true, but it is really an instance of the *extrapolation error* and a failure to consider all the possible outcomes of the situation. That requires System Two thinking. Many things could happen with our doomed car: it could slow down, break down, turn around, or stop.

The unaware investor is the great extrapolator. If the market has been going up steadily, it "feels" like it will continue. As an advisor, I've heard people say, "I had $100,000 invested four years ago and that has doubled. I now have $200,000. In 12 years, I should have $1.2 million." When the market has been trending down, I'll hear the opposite: "My $1 million became $800,000 in a year. At that rate, I will be broke in 10 years." We think these thoughts all the time and need to be aware how harmful they can be.

Even scientists fall prey to embarrassing extrapolation errors. Many discredited scientific facts were extrapolated and many of them continue to be believed. Acid rain and the hole in the ozone would have both killed us all, as would overpopulation as explained in *The Population Bomb* in 1968. All of these fantasies were invented and believed by leading scientists.

The Gambler's Fallacy

When it comes to probability, a lack of understanding can lead to incorrect assumptions and predictions about the onset of events. That is the basis for the *gambler's fallacy*.

One of the most famous disclaimers in finance is that "past performance is no guarantee of future results." Even with that warning, it's common to use what happened in the past to construct an idea of what will happen the future. How many of you have played roulette at a casino under the premise that a string of red increases the likelihood of a black outcome? The fact is, though, that a random event does not change the probability that certain events will occur in the future.

Flip a coin that lands on "heads" 20 times in a row, and you might predict it's due to land on "tails." Probability tells us that it's still a 50/50 shot, assuming it's not a rigged coin. If there were a disclaimer on coin flipping, it would say "Past flips have no influence on future flips."

Investors or traders can easily fall prey to the gambler's fallacy. For example, some investors believe that they should liquidate a position after it has gone up in a series of subsequent trading sessions because they don't believe that the position is likely to continue going up. Conversely, other investors might hold on to a stock that has fallen in multiple sessions because they view further declines as improbable. Just because a stock has gone up on six consecutive trading sessions does not mean that it is less likely to go up on during the next session. It's important to understand that in the case of independent events, the odds of any specific outcome happening on the next chance remains the same *regardless of what preceded it.*

Hindsight Bias

I can't begin to tell you how many times I hear this one, which is related to *should statements* discussed earlier. Hindsight bias is what makes us say, "I knew that stock was going to go up." Here's the cure: Thinking rationally, if you knew the stock was going to go up, you would have purchased it 100% of the time. The fact that you didn't purchase the stock tells you that you didn't know, so don't beat yourself up.

Should you spend time and emotional energy kicking yourself for not having supernatural powers? "I should have known that was going to happen" is another hindsight thought. Really? If there really are psychics, why aren't they buying stocks instead of selling readings? My point here is that not even psychics are psychic, so why should you be? This is where I bring out an old copy of the *Wall Street Journal* and ask people if they want to have a pity party over all the stuff they didn't know in advance. The fact is you *don't have to know*. You will become wealthy using wisdom, mindfulness and control of your thoughts.

Outcome bias is a variation of hindsight bias. When the outcome is known, it is impossible to go back and ascertain your original state of mind. For instance, when a person dies in surgery, the result is going to bring an outcry that it was too risky and *should have* been known by the surgeon. It may become a news event, especially when a celebrity is the deceased patient. After the surgery, it is impossible to know how confident the loved ones or the medical professionals *were*. As investors, we do this all the time. Not every stock you are confident about will go up—and in some cases, you will wonder how you ever thought it would, since the results seem so clear *after the outcome is known*. A good example of outcome bias is my confidence I had in the prospect that the trucking industry would be revolutionized by the natural gas engine. It never happened.

Bandwagon

You might also hear this called *argument from common sense* or *argumentum ad populum*. This is a fallacy that, because "everyone" supposedly thinks or does something, it must be right. For example, "Everyone knows that undocumented aliens ought to be kicked out!" A variation on this is lying with statistics: "Surveys show that over 75% of Americans believe Senator Smith is not telling the truth. For anyone with half a brain, that conclusively proves he's a dirty liar!"

I Wish I Had a Magic Wand Fallacy

Here, we have the fallacy of regretfully (and falsely) proclaiming oneself powerless to change a bad or objectionable situation. For example, "What can we do about high gas prices? As Secretary of Energy, I wish I had a magic wand, but I don't." Using the *magic wand fallacy* implies that a magic wand is the only solution to the problem. It helps take the responsibility that you could have had for a decision seem futile when it is not.

If you were a parent, you may have wielded this one as follows: "No, you can't quit piano lessons. I wish I had a magic wand and could teach you piano overnight, but I don't. So, like it or not, you have to keep on practicing." Putting it that way ignores the possibility that the child may not want or need to learn piano or that you could establish a way to help your child more if you wished to.

Appeal to Heaven

This fallacy can be particularly dangerous: asserting that God (or another higher power) has ordered, supports, or approves of your position or actions, so no further justification is required and no serious challenge is possible. Unfortunately, this is how many wars start. Think about terrorists who believe they have a mandate from their god to kill all of us. When I encounter clients who want to pray about their investment decisions, it's a tough one for me; I pray and believe in prayer, but I don't believe God intervenes to help his people pick stocks or hockey games or lotto numbers. My recommendation is to pray for wisdom, have peace with the decision, then leave it to God.

If you are trying to decide between buying Johnson & Johnson or Starbucks, I don't believe it will help to ask God to choose. If it worked that way, all charities would have billions and they'd never have a need for donations.

Confirmation Bias

Confirmation bias is looking for or seeing only what confirms your beliefs, and ignoring or undervaluing the things that don't or are contradictory. You'll also hear it called *selective thinking*. For example, if someone believes in UFOs, the believer will usually put a lot of faith in articles that show evidence for UFOs and ignore articles that argue that aliens have not visited Earth.

This is a serious problem in investment selection. We get an idea that we are excited about, and use a *heuristic* to find the idea. Then we go back it up with specific facts. Google has compounded the problem: I can find 10 articles that say a particular stock is going much higher and 10 articles that say it's going much lower. If you want to make it worse, you can embed confirmation bias in the search: "Reasons why Wal-Mart stock will perform well."

Negativity Bias

Let's face it: We live in a sensationalist society in which scare tactics and negative headlines garner the most attention. Scientists theorize that we perceive negative news to be more important than positive news. The risk—for stock-market bears and for humans as a whole—is the tendency to dwell on bad news rather than embrace good news. That's compounded by the fact that the stock market is widely considered to be a leading indicator. Negativity bias will frequently leave you on the wrong side of history.

Sunk-Cost Error

In economics and business decision-making, a *sunk cost* is a cost that has already been incurred and cannot be recovered. (In contrast, *prospective costs* are future costs that may be incurred or changed if an action is taken.)

In a 1985 study, "The Psychology of Sunk Cost," researchers Hal Arkes and Catherine Blumer asked subjects to assume they had spent $100 on a ticket for a ski trip in Michigan, then, several weeks later found and bought a ticket for a ski trip they'd enjoy more in Wisconsin for $50. Just as the second ticket was purchased, the subjects discovered they were both for the same weekend—and the tickets couldn't be refunded or sold. Forced to choose, did they select the $100 good vacation, or the $50 great vacation? You guessed it: More people chose the higher-priced trip rather than the more enjoyable one.

The sunk-cost fallacy can be a killer for your portfolio, because it means hanging on to positions that you have spent a lot of time and money on. Because of your perceived sunk costs, you are reluctant to see that some other investment might be better.

In traditional microeconomic theory, only prospective (future) costs are relevant to an investment decision. Traditional economics proposes that economic actors should not let sunk costs influence their decisions, but rather make decisions on their own merits.

A related mistake is *escalation of commitment*, which was first described by Barry M. Staw in his 1976 paper, "Knee deep in the big muddy: A study of escalating commitment to a chosen course of action." This compounds the sunk cost error in the ways that are familiar to us in sayings such as "Throwing good money after bad" or "In for a dime, in for a dollar." It's also part of the multilevel marketing industry, when distributors chase past purchases to "keep the dream alive" by buying more and more of the product being marketed.

Cherry Picking

Salespeople will always remind you of the good features of a product and not talk about the bad. In the investment industry, *cherry picking* comes in the form of a broker citing past successful stock ideas and ignoring the bad ones.

Errors Illustrated

The following paragraph is a typical broker pitch, in which I have marked the fallacies and thinking errors involved.

"Hi Bob, this is Gordon Gecko calling from downtown Manhattan with a stock tip for you today. I called you last week about Go-Diapers, Inc., the company that makes diapers that dissolve after they are in the landfill. When I called you last time the stock was $3.00 and today, just two weeks later, it's at $4.00 (*hindsight bias/*

should statement). That's more than a 30% gain! Every environmental scientist (*appeal to authority/bandwagon*) we have spoken to is positive about these being the diapers of the future (*confirmation bias*). The stock has now gone up 6 weeks in a row (*gambler's fallacy*)! It was only $2.00 a month ago. At this rate, can you imagine where it might be at the end of the year (*extrapolation error*)? The last time our analysts saw a stock pick like this, several of our clients made five times their investment (*cherry picking*)."

Obviously, this is an extreme example to illustrate the principles. But now that you know the signs, you hopefully will avoid buying into the stock-market equivalent of a loaded diaper.

CHAPTER 16

The Key Is Your World View

"Astrologers, palmists, and crystal-ball gazers are scorned while professional economists are heralded for their scientific achievements. Yet the academics are no less mystical in trying to predict the direction of interest rates, economic growth, and the stock market."

—Graeme Littler

Let's consider Bob. He's 62 years old, graduated high school in 1972, and finished college in 1977. He currently has $2 million in his retirement plan and $500,000 in other investments and savings. Bob wants to retire, but he can't. He is a regular listener of nightly news, sometimes until 10, and then switches to the local news. He looks at financial media daily and reads articles related to his stock holdings. Bob and his wife need about $8,000 per month after taxes to continue their lifestyle. His salary is $200,000, of which $25,000 goes into his 401(k), $40,000 goes to taxes, and $10,000 to charity every year.

Bob hates his job and actually wants to do something different. But Bob has a problem. Bob is absolutely convinced that financial Armageddon is just around the corner—a thought he has held for almost 40 years. In essence, Bob is the Elevator Guy from chapter two, who assumes that the fact that the elevator hasn't fallen is proof that it's due to happen. He knows things have been bad in the past, but nothing as bad as what's happening in today's world. He really wants to own some gold but hasn't purchased it because it pays no income, it is expensive to store, and Home Depot won't take a chunk of it in exchange for new hardwood flooring.

When Bob watches the news he becomes anxious about his investments, and, since he feels so worried, there must be a danger out there somewhere. Emotional reasoning is his thinking error.

A host of fallacies and biases haunt him. Bob's fortune-teller error is "The government is printing money hand over fist! The end is near!" He discounts the positive by ignoring four decades of rising stock prices in his own lifetime. (He should be averaging around 10% on his retirement account returns since he is currently invested in stocks. But his average is only 2.9%.)

Part of the problem is that Bob—like many professional economists—has predicted 18 of the last three recessions, and the gambler's fallacy tells him that it has been too long since the last recession. So, once again Bob is on the sidelines. The market is down 22%. Everything he hears on TV says we are going way lower. In fact, the same people who said we were going higher three months ago are now the ones convinced we are going lower—financial journalists with great charisma but terrible instincts. Because Bob bobs in and out of the market, he misses a lot of up days. The chart below shows you how much you would lose by being "on the sidelines" during the best days over 20 years.

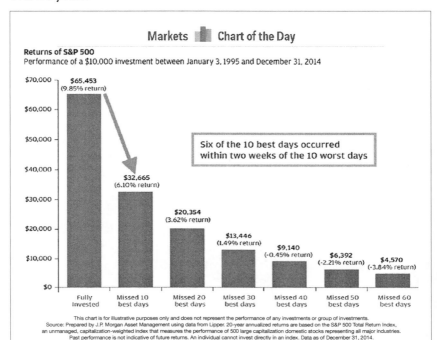

Markets — Chart of the Day

Returns of S&P 500
Performance of a $10,000 investment between January 3, 1995 and December 31, 2014

Six of the 10 best days occurred within two weeks of the 10 worst days

- Fully Invested: $65,453 (9.85% return)
- Missed 10 best days: $32,665 (6.10% return)
- Missed 20 best days: $20,354 (3.62% return)
- Missed 30 best days: $13,446 (1.49% return)
- Missed 40 best days: $9,140 (-0.45% return)
- Missed 50 best days: $6,392 (-2.21% return)
- Missed 60 best days: $4,570 (-3.84% return)

This chart is for illustrative purposes only and does not represent the performance of any investments or group of investments. Source: Prepared by J.P. Morgan Asset Management using data from Lipper. 20-year annualized returns are based on the S&P 500 Total Return Index, an unmanaged, capitalization-weighted index that measures the performance of 500 large capitalization domestic stocks representing all major industries. Past performance is not indicative of future returns. An individual cannot invest directly in an index. Data as of December 31, 2014.

We can't help Bob until he turns off the TV and realizes that financial media is entertainment, not advice.

My first memory of thinking "the end is near" began in 1970, when a neighbor gave me a copy of *The Late Great Planet Earth* by evangelist Hal Lindsey. That book, the biggest selling non-fiction book since the Bible, has sold over 35 million copies. The end was going to come soon…1988 at the latest. It didn't end, So he wrote another bestseller *The 1980s: Countdown to Armageddon.* As far as I know, the world has not ended yet, so you'd imagine he has been discredited and shunned by all the people he scared, right? WRONG! At 86, Lindsey has his own TV show, continues to write bestsellers, and has a popular newsletter. He is also on his fourth wife. The fact that he should have zero credibility based on his past predictions does not deter his growing fan base, and he has even spawned dozens of similar "end time ministries." When you look up "wrong" in the dictionary, there should be a picture of Hal Lindsey.

What does a doomsday preacher have to do with investing? Because stock-market-doomsday pundits are made from the same mold. Fear is a very easy, lucrative sale. Tune in to talk radio and a high percent of the ads warn about stock-market horrors and recommend gold and annuities as the solution. In the late '90s, the doomsday machine was at full speed with the certain disaster to be caused by Y2k. I got so tired of hearing about it, I wrote a book, *Y2k We're OK—Why the Millennium Bug Won't Bite.* At the time, there were dozens of books warning us about the dire situation we were in, but I knew of only one other book that threw water on Y2k. Neither of us sold many books of course.

With the turn of the millennium, the Y2k bug was coming to get us.
I got so tired of hearing about it, I wrote a book:
Y2k We're OK—Why the Millennium Bug Won't Bite.

Here's a question that will give you insight on your potential for investment success: Is the world generally getting better or worse?

Before you answer, consider that the concept of accumulating money into a big pile and never working again was science fiction for most human beings prior to the 20th century. For thousands of years, we were grateful to get up and feed our family every day, keep them sheltered, healthy, etc. Today, it can ruin our week if our fantasy football picks don't perform well.

If you think the good old days were better, I understand. We were young and that's how memory works. We get nostalgic over old times, and baby boomers look back fondly on their childhoods in the '50s and '60s. But, in general, we continue to progress. No matter what problems you have, you would never trade in the house on the cul de sac for life in a village of mud huts, under constant threat of barbarian hordes.

A Tale of Four Decades

Let's take a trip down memory lane—and maybe earlier, if you were born before 1975. The following thoughts are *random and not in order of importance*. Thanks to Nick Murray for letting me borrow much of this history. I added a few of my memories also.

1975

Saturday Night Live premieres in October. President Ford escapes two assassination attempts. Sara Jane Moore and Lynette "Squeaky" Fromme hold the distinction of being the only two women who have ever attempted to assassinate an American president, both of their attempts being on Gerald Ford and both taking place in California within three weeks of one another. Fromme was a follower of Charles Manson and Moore was fascinated with the Patty Hearst kidnapping. The .38 revolver she fired was off by 6 inches. Moore, reportedly a crack shot with her own pistol, had obtained this one the morning of the shooting. With her own gun, history may have been changed and Nelson Rockefeller would have been president.

Margaret Thatcher becomes the first woman to lead the Britain's Conservative party. We link up with a Soviet spacecraft, and a beautiful ten-cent postage stamp is issued to commemorate the event.

- Global population: 4.1 billion (50% live in extreme poverty)
- U.S. population: 216 million
- U.S. real GDP: $5.49 trillion

- **S&P 500 year end close 90.19**
- **S&P total earnings per share: $34.01**
- **S&P total dividends per share: $15.72**

1985

Gorbachev comes to power in the Soviet Union and meets with President Reagan. Four years later, the Iron Curtain fell and communism as we knew it was added to the ash-heap of human history. The Internet domain name system is established. I had not even heard of the Internet. I pass my first (Series 6) Securities exam in August of 1985. The first of 6.

The first version of Windows becomes available, and I would not understand the term *Windows* until 1990. I know that because I bought my first computer in 1990 and the guy asked me if I wanted DOS or Windows. I knew nothing other than that DOS was cheaper. It cost me more than $1500 in 1990 dollars or about one month's salary from the job I had out of college. Had to switch to Windows two years later.

The first successful human heart transplant takes place. We now do 2,000 of these a year with increasingly good outcomes. You may find yourself fly fishing in Jackson Hole next to a 75-year-old with a heart transplant. That would be Dick Cheney. You may golf with the PGA touring pro Erik Compton, who took up golf at 12 after his first heart transplant because he couldn't play football. He has earned over $4 million in tour winnings.

The song of the year is "We are the World." In the greatest marketing catastrophe since the Edsel, the Coca-Cola Company changes the formula of Coke.

A first class U.S. postage stamp is 22 cents.

- Global population: 4.85 billion
- U.S. population: 238 million
- U.S. real GDP: $7.71 trillion
- **S&P year end close: 211.28**
- **S&P total earnings per share: $15.68**
- **S&P total dividends per share: $8.20**

1995

The Oklahoma City bombing is the worst case of domestic terrorism in US history. O.J. Simpson's trial begins, becomes a national obsession, and ten months later ends in acquittal. We still did not have access to Internet updates at our office. We drove over to my colleague's house and watched the announcement of the verdict. We stood in disbelief as "the Juice" was found not guilty of the murders, but has been incarcerated in Nevada for robbery since 2008. According to the most recent news reports, he could be released in 2017.

Acid rain and depletion of the ozone were going to kill us all. Reports of blind rabbits and fish were regularly heard. The Black Forest in Germany would be toast within 10 to 20 years. Those two panics also ended up on that trash heap of crises that never were.

Israeli Prime Minister Yitzhak Rabin is assassinated. The Rock and Roll Hall of Fame opens in Cleveland and Jerry Garcia dies. A postage stamp costs 32 cents.

- Global population: 5.7 billion
- U.S. population: 266 million
- U.S. real GDP: $10.28 trillion
- **S&P year end close: 615.93**
- **S&P total earnings per share: $37.70**
- **S&P total dividends per share: $14.17**

2005

Hurricane Katrina devastates an American landmass larger than Great Britain. Saddam Hussein goes on trial for his life and loses. (He gets executed on December 30, 2006. An amateur video shot using a camera phone from a staircase leading up to the gallows surfaced, contained low-quality footage of the entire hanging. The amateur footage, unlike the official footage, included sound; witnesses could be heard taunting Saddam at the gallows. The video is historic in that it demonstrated the amazing power of technology to deliver truth. (Propaganda from media and government would never be as easy).

July 7 becomes London's 9/11, as coordinated attacks on bus and subways claim 52 lives. Pope John Paul ll dies. Kim Jong-il shows off his nuclear weaponry. A U.S. postage stamp costs 37 cents.

- Global population: 6.5 billion (one in three in extreme poverty)
- U.S. population: 296 million
- U.S. gross GDP: $14.37 trillion
- **S&P 500 year end close: 1248.29**
- **S&P total earnings per share: $76.45**
- **S&P total dividends per share: $22.38**

2015

An Islamic faction called *ISIS* casts the Middle East into chaos. (As if the Middle East isn't always in chaos.) ISIS carries out terrorist attacks in Paris and elsewhere. To me, this always triggers the question, "Tell me again, what do they want?"

The U.S. reaches an accord with Iran on nuclear development. Our great philosopher and baseball legend Yogi Berra dies. I have a signed baseball from him that will now be more important than ever. And as Yogi said, when you look back on events over the past nothing changes much. "It is like déjà vu all over again."

- A first class U.S. postage stamp is 49 cents.
- Global population: 7.29 million (less than 10% in extreme poverty)
- U.S. population: 322 million
- U.S. real GDP: $17.97 trillion
- **S&P 500 year end close: 2043.94**
- **S&P total earnings per share: $88.00**
- **S&P total dividends per share: $43.00**

This, then, is the tale of four decades:

The global population is up nearly 80%, with extreme poverty going from one in two people to one in ten. Wave upon wave of new middle-class consumers are appearing.

U.S. population grows by half, and we gain a new person about every 14 seconds due to births and migration. Still, we have unimaginable room to grow. Population density per square mile in the U.S. is 85, compared to 300 in France, 590 in Germany, 680 in Great Britain, and 870 in Japan.

We have staggering natural resources, with mineral rights vested to the owner. One hundred years of known hydrocarbon reserves sit under us—making the end of fossil fuels a fear that is full of thinking errors, including fortune-telling and discounting the positive. Believers are the modern-day version of the handwringers who thought the world would go dark due to whale blubber running out.

Real GDP more than tripled, on only a 50% population increase—meaning GDP per person has soared.

The S&P 500 rose more than 20 times, on an earnings increase in excess of 15 times and a dividend boost of 12 times. Far more significantly, these gains have to be measured against the increase in consumer prices, which was four and a half times. This is the greatest accretion of real wealth by the greatest number of people in the history of the world.

If your brain is telling you it can't continue, don't bet on it. What are the megatrends that underpin this spectacular economic and financial progress? There are two, and they create a virtuous cycle: 1) the spread of the free market, as liberty has vanquished most forms of communism and extreme socialism during this time, and 2) the exponential progress in information technology. (Today, a middle school child carries in his backpack more computing power than the largest mainframe computer in the world in 1975. This cycle continues apace.)

But aren't we peaking now, or won't we in the near future? I will leave you with this quote from Lowell Wood, who recently became the largest holder of U.S. patents. He passed Thomas Edison's 1805 patented inventions in June of 2015, and he has more than 3,000 waiting to be reviewed. He is undoubtedly the inventor of our era. He is 74 years old. When asked if humankind had topped out in technology, this is what he had to say: "It's irrational. It's frankly illiterate to not be optimistic. We're going to see a blossoming across essentially every front, unprecedented in human technological history. This is not something that's hoped for. This is baked in the cake."

I hope you will go now and buy some shares in the greatest businesses in the world. When I first found out that I could buy the same shares in Microsoft that Bill Gates owns or the same shares in Starbucks that Howard Schultz has, I thought it was too good to be true. It's not. You just have to get your brain out of your way and start building wealth.

ABOUT THE AUTHOR

Craig Verdi, CFP® is president and founder of Verdi Wealth Planning, Inc., and has worked extensively in the field of financial management since 1985.

A graduate of Washington State University, Craig holds the CERTIFIED FINANCIAL PLANNER™ certification through the American College. He holds the series 7, 6, 24, 26, 63, and 65 securities registrations through Commonwealth Financial Network. His first book was *Y2K, We're OK: Why the Millennium Bug Won't Bite.*

Craig has two boys, Dominic and Christopher, and currently resides in southeast Boise, Idaho, and Scottsdale, Arizona. He enjoys spending time with his family and is an avid fly fisherman, golfer, and bird hunter as well. Craig is also the former president of the board for the Boise Rescue Mission.

Securities and Advisory Services offered through Commonwealth Financial Network, Member FINRA/SIPC, a Registered Investment Adviser.

RECOMMENDED READING

One Up on Wall Street, Peter Lynch

The Intelligent Investor, Benjamin Graham

Stocks for the Long Run, Jeremy Siegel

Anything written by Warren Buffett on investing,
including his annual reports to Berkshire Hathaway investors—
which are a great way to learn about how Buffett's mind works.
They are readily available online.

You Are Not Your Brain, Jeffrey Schwartz, M.D.

The Mind and the Brain, Jeffrey Schwartz, M.D.

The Brain that Changes Itself, Norman Doidge, M.D.

Thinking, Fast and Slow, Daniel Kahneman

Feeling Good – The New Mood Therapy, David Burns, M.D.

◆

How I Think about Stocks: My Initial Screening Process

This was an email I sent to my son, Chris. I had never put down in writing the process I go through in my head. There are a lot of other things that come into play, but this will give you a good idea of the basic process I use.

Use the "My Portfolio" feature on Yahoo Finance. It is great, and shows most of the information you would ever want.

Let's start with Coke (KO), a huge company widely held by almost all big-cap managers.

I know up front Coke is a stock I know I want to own: A giant historic distribution system. Largest Beverage Company in the world, etc. A consumable product not economically sensitive. Addictive, cheap to make, the perfect Buffett stock. And it is totally understandable. We serve it at the office and drink generic at home although we drink a lot of Coke products.

1. I go to PROFILE. I want to see what they do that I don't know. I find out that Coke just doesn't sell Coke. They continue to grow by expanding product. I see a lot of products I don't know and some of them I may personally know are "hot."

The company primarily offers sparkling beverages and still beverages. Its sparkling beverages include nonalcoholic ready-to-drink beverages with carbonation, such as carbonated energy drinks, and carbonated waters and flavored waters. The company's still beverages comprise nonalcoholic beverages without carbonation, including noncarbonated waters, flavored and enhanced waters, noncarbonated energy drinks, juices and juice drinks, ready-to-drink teas and coffees, and sports drinks. It also provides flavoring ingredients, sweeteners, beverage ingredients, and fountain syrups, as well as powders for purified water products. In addition, the company licenses its technologies and trademarks to suppliers and third parties. The Coca-Cola Company sells its products primarily under Coca-Cola, Diet Coke, Coca-Cola Light, Coca-Cola Zero, Fanta, Sprite, Minute Maid, Georgia, Powerade, Del Valle, Schweppes, Aquarius, Minute Maid Pulpy, Dasani, Simply, Glacéau, Vitaminwater, Bonaqua/Bonaqa, Ayataka, Gold Peak, I LOHAS, and FUZE TEA brand names. The company offers its beverage products through a network of company-owned or controlled bottling and distribution operators, as well as through independent bottling partners, distributors, wholesalers, and retailers. The Coca-Cola Company was founded in 1886 and is headquartered in Atlanta, Georgia.

2. Second I look at price. I look at the chart only to get a rough idea of how it has gotten to here.

3. Then I look at the P/E ratio and then the dividend, if any.

4. I take the dividend—3.5%—and add it to my predicted growth rate. Growth rate is only about 5%. So I get a total of 8.5%. I compare that to the P/E ratio. I want the growth rate plus dividend to be higher than the P/E. If there is no dividend, then it is just the growth rate. I see the P/E is 25. Normally, in a no-name company, this would be a stopper. But I know that companies like this command higher prices (higher "multiples") because they are so stable and raise dividends decade after decade, which is huge in a long-term investment. Then I want to know what P/E it has commanded historically. This is a *premium P/E stock,* but I don't know by how much. I may Google "historic P/E for KO" to give a number to the premium. I may think, this is only a total of 9 with a 25 P/E. That sounds rotten, but depends on historic P/E during downturns.

5. Retired shares. This is the effect of share buybacks, which are huge—you can find this on Value Line, which shows active shares year by year. Decreasing shares is positive because you end up with more earnings per share. Share buybacks are like tax-free dividends.

6. PEG. Popularized by Peter Lynch, this ratio shows the P/E–Growth rate. Lower is better.

7. Book value. Benjamin Graham wanted 1.3 or lower, but that is not as common now. Each industry is different.

8. Payout ratio. If the stock pays dividends, it should not be paying out too much. This is tricky. This should be below 50%. If a company is yielding 2% and has a payout ratio of 15% that should be good. Trial and error to get the hang of it. Remember that some companies will be much higher, like utilities, BDCs, MLP's etc.

9. Dividend history. I use Dividata.com to get the dividend history. I want to see a good history of hiking dividends.

10. I read the analysis by Morningstar, Value Line, and Argus. They all have a good reputation, and Value Line is often cited as the reason why you should not buy index funds. They have killed the index.

11. I have to like it. I have to be excited about the idea. For instance, if I don't like the prospects due to competition, I don't bite. I recently looked at a promising company, but passed on it due to the fact that they no patented products and could get wiped out by huge companies.

12. I look at "key statistics," specifically debt, cash per share, and price/sales. You want a debt/equity ratio that is low. Below 50% is generally good. But if a company is hot and borrowing to

facilitate fast growth a higher rate may be OK. With price to sale, lower is better. Sometimes cash per share is 50% of price. Peter Lynch calls this an asset sale, when the company has more cash and assets than the price of the stock, or they have hidden assets like land.

13. I look at the balance sheet for hidden holdings in real estate, etc. I also look for phony assets like excessive "blue sky."

14. I like to look at insider buying and selling. Read Lynch on this. I also like to know who owns it. If a mutual fund manager whom I admire has a lot of it, I like that.

Of course, I couldn't care less about moving averages, trading ranges, charts, etc. Nor do I care about the effect of voodoo, sunspots, or astrology on stock prices. If everything looks good, I buy. I almost never sell a dividend raiser. But you have to check in on your original thesis every quarter or 6 months to make sure no major problems have come up.

Is Investing Gambling?
Lessons from Las Vegas

Stock market investing is not gambling. But you can make it gambling if you choose. I believe the majority of people who invest do it just as if they *are* gambling. They really don't know why they are winning or losing. They may think of stocks going up is just good luck, even as the Dow is up 10- or 20-fold in their lifetimes. Thirty-five years ago I was on a gambling quest. I quickly learned all the odds of the games in Las Vegas. I knew from the start that every game in Nevada was fixed in favor of the house, with the exception of poker and blackjack. So, I had to choose one of them. I chose blackjack. The odds of making a living are far better in poker, but at the time, there was a lot of excitement about the relatively new concept that blackjack could be beaten. I was a college student at the time and it would not have mattered. I wasn't going to be a card player of any kind it turned out. Today, I can hardly get through a game of *Go Fish*.

Poker is a conundrum for casinos. The winners are equal to the losers at the table. There is no way for the casino to put themselves in the winner's seat. The casino isn't betting against you with their money. It is completely unique in that way. The casinos only make money by taking a percentage of each pot and creating an attractive venue for players. Not much money in that. That's why you don't see a lot of poker in casinos.

The odd thing about blackjack is that the casinos set the rules and then realized, with better math, that the odds were actually against them. The first person to popularize that idea was Edward Thorpe, who wrote *Beat the Dealer* in 1959. Now the public knew or could know that blackjack was *beatable and legal*. That must have put the casinos in a tailspin, don't you think? What would happen to them, once the public learned they could beat them at their own game? You know what happened. Not much. There are a few stories of the card counter here and there, but it really hasn't been an issue for casinos. True, they have kicked people out and have beat up a few people occasionally, but not nearly as much as you may think. The game continues to be hugely popular and profitable for the casinos.

To beat blackjack you have to be able to do a couple of things. First, you must play a perfect strategy. You have to hit when you should hit, and stand when you should stand, *by the math*. You need to split cards and double down according to the math. If you can do all this, you can almost even the odds with the house, about 49.5 for you, 51.5 for them. When you sit down and wing it, go by feelings, think you are getting hot, or any other superstition, you put yourself at a huge disadvantage. The house makes more than 20% on these players. They are just doing it for fun and they think they may get lucky—and they might.

Second, you must keep track or "count" the number of low-numbered cards in the deck. When the deck is rich in high-numbered cards (10-King), the advantage for the perfect-strategy player swings in favor of the player. This gives the player about a 1.5% advantage.

So for me, I could never sit at another table once I knew this information. If I didn't keep perfect strategy and perfect track of the cards, how could I plop down my hard-earned money, especially as a college student? I couldn't so I made sure I played right every time. I was winning, but it took so much time and concentration, I gave up. I could have used a lot bigger bankroll also, but that wouldn't have made me keep playing. I realized it was not for me. Knowing what I know, I have not sat down at a blackjack table in more than 30 years. To me that seems a natural response. But to many might say, "Why not try it? You might win!" The easiest bets come in games like golf, because most people are worse players than they think. Overconfidence and superstition are very expensive. I don't recommend practicing either of them.

The casinos make huge profits when people who logically know they will lose continue to play. Of all the quirks of human nature, this one seems most peculiar. I understand the desire to make money. To give up your money in a rigged game has never made sense to me. As your friends return from Nevada, you can expect the usual answer about their gambling: "I think I paid for the trip" or "I have won more than I have lost." Las Vegas was built on people who sincerely believe that.

The game of poker might be a better choice. The winners grind down the losers and the losers keep coming back for more. You don't win long term in poker by luck. If there wasn't enough luck to win in the short run, no bad players would play. But there is always a chance. It's the lucky winning that keeps them coming back. Most people who consistently lose don't think they are lucky when they win.

The reason that poker is so popular, besides being great fun for some, is that there is always the illusion of victory, even when you are just getting lucky. You may come home for weeks or months from your hometown game and be a winner, even if you are a horrible player. It is just a matter of time until it catches up with you.

Lou Piccioni, an investor and poker enthusiast, has some thoughts on how poker is similar to investing:

The skills involved are similar:

- Unthinkable patience. One must be able to fold hand after hand. Many players can't go more than ten hands without losing patience.

- Discipline. One has to be disciplined at the table as well as away from the table. This means not drinking large amounts of alcohol, getting plenty of sleep, picking the right games and having a game plan. People who lead chaotic lives are usually chaotic at the poker table. On the other hand you don't want to be a complete "rock." A rock in poker is someone who sits there, hand after hand, waiting for an ideal hand that they "know" they can win. Rocks don't take enough risk to win.

- Understanding the game. As with the market, if you don't understand it and just invest in what looks good (by using hunches and tips from "friends") you will not fare well in the long run.

- Knowing when to take risks. This is a hallmark of the good poker player and investor. Taking some risk must be done to make profits, but they must be calculated risks. Sometimes the line between being reckless and taking calculated risks is blurred. This can only come with experience.

- Controlling emotions. Many players as well as investors lack the ability to do this. That is where this book comes in.

- Sufficient bankroll, or in the case of investing: capital. You must be able to stay in the game long enough to reap the benefits of the odds that will come your way if you are a good player.

You Can Be the Casino!

Do you want to be the casino or the gambler? The casino is set up in advance to win. All systems are calculated precisely to run at a set profit. Not all of them are successful but if they are well run and well-funded, they cannot lose.

Don't confuse a bull market with brains. You can get lucky in the market also. But you don't need to get lucky. You are now the casino! The game is rigged in your favor! Just wait it out and watch the earnings come in. The market goes up over time, not down, whereas gamblers lose over time. The casino does not need luck.

The Rule of 72

The rule of 72 is something important to carry with you in your mind. It is simply this: To know how long it takes your money to double, take the rate at which you expect it to grow and divide it into 72. Since stocks have averaged around 10% (with dividends reinvested), you can start with that. 72/10 = 7.2 That 7.2 is the number of years it takes your money to double. It works with any divisor.

This is a great rule of thumb to have in your head when thinking about your financial situation. You may be a 30 year old with $50,000 invested, and you wonder how much it will be worth when you are 60 years old. Using the rule of 72, you can do this in your head or with a pen and paper to see how many times your 50 grand will "flip" or double.

Your money will double in 7.2 years at 10%, but let's say your money will double every 7 years to make it easier to do without a calculator. The way I would do it is by thinking "OK, I am 30 so when I am 37 it will double for the first time and be $100,000." Pretty cool.

Then 7 years later, when I am 44, it will double again and be $200,000.

At 51, that's $400,000.

At 58, that's $800,000.

At 65, that's $1,600,000.

In theory, that means having $1.6 million just by resisting the urge to touch it—and that's not including any subsequent additions.

Now what if you'd started at 23? Well, that's easy. The money would have an extra seven years to double, making the figures $1.6 million at 58 and $3.2 million at 65.

Clearly, the cost of waiting is enormous. When talking about retirement, a lot of people are going to start next year after they get "caught up." What happens if a 30-year-old couple decides to wait a year before starting a $5,000-a-year investment plan? They're robbing their 65-year-old selves of $160,000!

Do a few examples for yourself. Put down the amount you have invested. Pick a few made up rates of return and divide into 72. It is a fun and easy way to get you excited about long term patience.

Today it is Dec. 28, 2016, and the Dow is around 19,500. I may be thinking that the market is overvalued. The rule of 72 is useful for me to go back to times in the past that in hindsight I thought were a reasonable price for stocks. 1986 is always memorable to me because I was new in the business and the market was going up and up and in August of 1986 was around 2600. "Black Monday" happened that year, with the Dow crashing to around 1,700 by January of 1987. I always thought that was a reasonable level. So to see if the market is out of whack today I can apply the rule of 72 to the Dow.

Again assuming 10% growth:

1987-2000
1994-4000 (7 year double)
2001-8000
2008-16,000
2015-32,000

So, for what it is worth, if the Dow averaged 10%, it would be worth well over the 20,000 level it is today. A return of around 8.5% from 1987 until now would put the Dow where it actually is at 20,000.

The Strange World of Technical Analysis/Chart Reading

"Previous support morphs into resistance. On the downside, the 1,815 level could be important for the long-term outlook. That's where an uptrend line drawn off the March 2009 low currently extends. Below that, the 1565-1575 area sticks out on the charts for two reasons: Where will the S&P 500 stop falling?

"The first key retracement level based on the Fibonacci, or "divine ratio," is around 1575. That represents a 38.2% retracement of the rally off the March 9, 2009 closing low of 676.53 to the May 21 high of 2,130.82. "The S&P 500's Oct. 9, 2007 closing high was 1,565, just before the Great Recession hit. That should have morphed into strong support."—Sample technical analysis

We hear of spooky things like the "divine ratio," the "Elliot wave theory," and the dreaded "death cross." These are all ridiculous names for a ridiculous practice: technical analysis/chart reading.

The results you get from technical analysis and chart reading would not vary from someone using astrology or tarot cards. Humans are pattern seekers. They want to see patterns, even when they are not there or not meaningful.

There has never been a study that could show that managing money by using charts gave superior long-term performance. Despite that fact, it is taught at some of the top US universities and around the world. Many schools have de-emphasized degrees in Technical Analysis, and the ones that remain are relegated to obscure, mostly online colleges.

A recent study by finance professors at Massey University in New Zealand examined more than 5,000 technical trading rules to see if they added value. The authors found "no evidence that the profits to the technical trading rules we consider are greater than those that might be expected due to random data variation."

Just tune into CNBC, Fox business or MSNBC business and you will have a chart reader give an opinion in short order. And the people talking about it do it with a straight face. Of course they do, they are true believers.

Following is an actual syllabus from an extension course from UCLA that teaches technical analysis.

Check out the terminology. You will learn about Fibonacci Levels and McClellan Oscillators. You will hear about some popular patterns that supposedly will make you rich. These include Piercing line/Dark Cloud Cover, Hammer/Hanging Man, and my favorite: Gravestone Doji/Dragon Fly Doji.

UCLA Extension

TECHNICAL STOCK MARKET & STOCK ANALYSIS

Date: April 6, 2013   **Duration:** 9:00 AM - 4:00 PM

Instructor: Andrew Lais, *Investment Executive & General Principal*

COURSE TOPICS AND AIM:

This course explores price and trading volume movements on various types of charts, including line, bar, candlestick, Point & Figure and Renko charts. You'll review annual, quarterly, monthly, weekly, daily and intra-day time segments. You are introduced to the most common technical indicators and oscillators and compare them on long-term versus short-term and ultra short-term charts. Topics include: the basics of 'support and resistance' levels, 'momentum buying', 'selling pressures', Fibonacci levels', regression channels', utilized in pinpointing entry and exit points.

Also covered are risk/reward ratios, entry/exit patterns, and dynamic stop-loss orders and how to set realistic price targets.

You will leave this class knowing what technical tools to look for and where to get the information from.

TEXT AND READINGS:

- *Japanese Candlestick Charting Techniques* by Steve Nison.
- *Beyond Candlesticks* by Steve Nison
- Chart School on the Internet: www.stockcharts.com
- *The Moving Average Convergence-Divergence* by Gerald Appel
- *New Concepts in Technical Trading Systems* by J. Welles Wilder, Jr.
- *Pattern for Profit: The McClellan Oscillator and Summation Index* by Sherman McClellan
- Key Ratios: Choose from either: www.smartmoney.com, or www.moneycentral.com or www.finance.yahoo.com

COURSE: 9:00 AM Introduction

- What is TA (Technical Analysis)?
- Why use TA?
- Some Fundamental requirements (Key Ratios)
- Price
- Time (Year, Quarter, Month, Week, 60 Minutes, 30 Minutes, 15 Minutes, 10 Minutes, 5 Minutes, 1 Minute, Second)
- Price History
- Trading Volume
- Bar Charts
- Line Charts
- Candlestick Charts

- Renko Charts
- Point & Figure Charts
- Heikin Ashi
- Trend
- Support and Resistance
- Oscillators
- Moving Averages
- Fibonacci Levels
- Regression Channels

(Continued)

Popular Candlestick Patterns
- Bullish/Bearish Belt Hold
- Bullish/Bearish Engulfing
- Piercing line/Dark Cloud Cover
- Morning Star/Evening Star
- Hammer/Hanging Man
- Doji
- Gravestone Doji/Dragon Fly Doji
- Shooting Star
- Long Legged Doji
- Doji Star
- Harami

Indicators including:
- TRIX
- MACD
- PPO (Percentage Price Oscillator)
- ADX (Average Directional Index)
- RSI (Relative Strength)
- STO (Stochastics)
- ROC (Rate of Change)
- Money Flow
- Williams %R
- Stochastics/RSI
- Commodity Cycle Index
- Accumulation/Distribution

Popular Chart Patterns
- Head and Shoulder Top/Bottoms
- Double Top and Bottoms
- Triple Top and Bottoms
- Rising/Falling Wedge
- Cup and Handle
- Flag and Pennant
- Symmetric Triangle
- Ascending Triangle
- Price Channels
- Gap Up
- Gap Down
- Leading Indicators vs. Lagging Ones